First World War
and Army of Occupation
War Diary
France, Belgium and Germany

33 DIVISION
98 Infantry Brigade
Royal Fusiliers (City of London Regiment)
19th Battalion
14 November 1915 - 29 February 1916

WO95/2427/3

The Naval & Military Press Ltd
www.nmarchive.com
Published in association with The National Archives

Published by

The Naval & Military Press Ltd

Unit 10 Ridgewood Industrial Park,

Uckfield, East Sussex,

TN22 5QE England

Tel: +44 (0) 1825 749494

www.naval-military-press.com

www.nmarchive.com

This diary has been reprinted in facsimile from the original. Any imperfections are inevitably reproduced and the quality may fall short of modern type and cartographic standards.

© **Crown Copyright**
Images reproduced by permission of The National Archives, London, England, 2015.

Contents

Document type	Place/Title	Date From	Date To
Heading	WO95/2427-3 19 Bn. Royal Fusiliers 1915 Dec-1916 May		
Heading	33rd Division 98th Infy Bde 19th Bn Royal Fus. Dec 1915-May 1916 Disbanded 21.5.16.		
Heading	98th Brigade 33rd Division. Battalion disembarked Calais 14.12.15. 19th Battalion Royal Fusiliers December 1915.		
War Diary	Tidworth. England	14/12/1915	14/12/1915
War Diary	Boulogne France	14/12/1915	14/12/1915
War Diary	Boulogne	15/12/1915	15/12/1915
War Diary	Thiennes.	16/12/1915	17/12/1915
War Diary	La Miquellerie Near Bvsnes.	19/12/1915	19/12/1915
War Diary	La Miquellerie	20/12/1915	20/12/1915
War Diary	Bethune	20/12/1915	25/12/1915
War Diary	Hinges	25/12/1915	25/12/1915
War Diary	Hingette and Avelette	26/12/1915	27/12/1915
War Diary	Billet	27/12/1915	29/12/1915
War Diary	Billet Essars.	30/12/1915	30/12/1915
Heading	98th Brigade. 33rd Division. 19th Battalion Royal Fusiliers January 1916		
War Diary	Brickstacks Sub-Section A1	01/01/1916	02/01/1916
War Diary	Near Tranches (Bricks Tacks) to Billet (Bethune)	02/01/1916	02/01/1916
War Diary	Billet (Bethune)	03/01/1916	05/01/1916
War Diary	Bethune	06/01/1916	07/01/1916
War Diary	Bethune Beuvry	08/01/1916	08/01/1916
War Diary	Billets Annequin South	09/01/1916	12/01/1916
War Diary	Annequin South	13/01/1916	15/01/1916
War Diary	Cambrin Trenches.	16/01/1916	16/01/1916
War Diary	Trenches	17/01/1916	24/01/1916
War Diary	Trenches and Bethune (Billets)	24/01/1916	24/02/1916
War Diary	Billets Bethune	25/02/1916	25/02/1916
War Diary	Billets Bethune to Annequin Fosse	26/02/1916	26/02/1916
War Diary	Annequin Fosse	27/02/1916	29/02/1916
War Diary	Trenches. Brickstacks.	30/01/1916	31/01/1916
Heading	98th Brigade 33rd Division Battalion Came Under G.H.Q. 27.2.16 19th Battalion Royal Fusiliers February 1916		
War Diary	Sub-Section A.I Cuinchy	01/02/1916	13/02/1916
War Diary	Cuincy Bethune	13/02/1916	13/02/1916
War Diary	Bethune	14/02/1916	20/02/1916
War Diary	Sub Section ZI	21/02/1916	29/02/1916
Heading	G.H.Q. Troops Came from 98th Brigade 33rd Division 27.2.16. 19th Battalion Royal Fusiliers March 1916		
War Diary	Racquinghem	01/03/1916	31/03/1916
Heading	Army Troops 19th Battalion The Royal Fusiliers April 1916		
War Diary	Racquinghem	01/04/1916	27/04/1916
War Diary	U Camp Etaples	28/04/1916	28/04/1916
War Diary	Etaples	29/04/1916	30/04/1916

Heading	Army Troops Disbanded 21st May 1916. 19th Battalion Royal Fusiliers May 1916		
War Diary	Etaples	01/05/1916	21/05/1916
Miscellaneous	Officer, i/c Records, Royal Fusiliers, Hounslow.	02/03/1916	02/03/1916
Miscellaneous	To. Capt. Atkinson. Are these Diaries with you, please?	21/02/1917	21/02/1917
Heading	WO95/2427-4 21 Bn Royal Fusiliers 1915 Nov-1916 Feb		
Heading	33 Div 98 Bde 21 Battn Royal Fus 1915 Nov-1916 Feb Disbanded April 1916		
Heading	98th Brigade 33rd Division. Battalion disembarked Calais 14.11.15. 21st Battalion Royal Fusiliers November 1915		
War Diary	Perham Down.	14/11/1915	14/11/1915
War Diary	Calais	14/11/1915	14/11/1915
War Diary	Boulogne	14/11/1915	17/11/1915
War Diary	Thiennes	18/11/1915	18/11/1915
War Diary	Cantrainne	19/11/1915	20/11/1915
War Diary	Bethune and A Section Trenches.	21/11/1915	25/11/1915
War Diary	Annequin North. and A Section BI Sub Section Trenches	26/11/1915	26/11/1915
War Diary	Annequin North and AI Sub Section BI Trenches	27/11/1915	27/11/1915
War Diary	Bethune.	28/11/1915	28/11/1915
War Diary	Les Harisoirs.	29/11/1915	30/11/1915
Heading	98th Brigade. 33rd Division. 21st Battalion Royal Fusiliers December 1915		
War Diary	Les Harisoirs.	01/12/1915	01/12/1915
War Diary	Les Harisoirs Epinette Festubert.	02/12/1915	02/12/1915
War Diary	Epinette Festubert	04/12/1915	04/12/1915
War Diary	Festubert & Epinette	05/12/1915	05/12/1915
War Diary	Festubert & Epinette. & Southern Subsectn Trenches.	06/12/1915	06/12/1915
War Diary	Southern Subsectn Trenches. Festubert.	07/12/1915	09/12/1915
War Diary	Southern Subsectn Trenches-Festubert.	10/12/1915	10/12/1915
War Diary	Gorre & Le Hamel	11/12/1915	11/12/1915
War Diary	Gorre & Le Hamel & Hingette.	12/12/1915	12/12/1915
War Diary	Hingette. L'Ecleme-Robecq.	13/12/1915	13/12/1915
War Diary	L'Ecleme.	14/12/1915	26/12/1915
War Diary	L'Ecleme Le Preul.	27/12/1915	27/12/1915
War Diary	Le Preol. B1. Subsectn. Trenches	28/12/1915	28/12/1915
War Diary	BI. Subsection.	29/12/1915	31/12/1915
Heading	98th Brigade. 33rd Division. 21st Battalion Royal Fusiliers January 1916		
War Diary	BI Subsection. & Annezin.	01/01/1916	01/01/1916
War Diary	Annezin.	02/01/1916	06/01/1916
War Diary	Bethune	07/01/1916	08/01/1916
War Diary	Annequin South. ZI & Z2 Subsections Trenches.	08/01/1916	09/01/1916
War Diary	Z Section Trenches.	10/01/1916	10/01/1916
War Diary	Z (1) (Left Coy) Z (2) Sub-Section of Trenches	10/01/1916	15/01/1916
War Diary	Sub Section of trenches	16/01/1916	16/01/1916
War Diary	Annequin. South	17/01/1916	22/01/1916
War Diary	Bethune	23/01/1916	31/01/1916
Heading	98th Brigade. 33rd Division. Battalion went to G.H.Q. 29.2.16. 21st Battalion Royal Fusiliers February 1916		
War Diary	BI. Subsection Trenches.	01/02/1916	14/02/1916
War Diary	BI. Subsection Trenches. & Rue D'Aire Bethune.	14/02/1916	21/02/1916
War Diary	Annequin South.	22/02/1916	22/02/1916
War Diary	Z2 Subsection Trenches.	23/02/1916	28/02/1916

War Diary	Rue D' Aire Bethune.	28/02/1916	28/02/1916
War Diary	Bethune & Wardrecques (G.H.Q.)	29/02/1916	29/02/1916

WO 95 2427/3
19 BN. ROYAL FUSILIERS
1915 DEC - 1916 MAY

33RD DIVISION
98TH INF'Y BDE

19th
20TH BN ROYAL FUS.
DEC MAY
NOV 1915 — 1916

DISBANDED 21.5.16
To B & C
27.2.16

98th Brigade
33rd Division.

Battalion disembarked Calais 14.12.15.

19th BATTALION

ROYAL FUSILIERS

DECEMBER 1915.

# WAR DIARY or INTELLIGENCE SUMMARY.

Army Form C. 2118.

Instructions regarding War Diaries and Intelligence Summaries are contained in F.S. Regs., Part II. and the Staff Manual respectively. Title pages will be prepared in manuscript.

(Erase heading not required.)

Hour, Date, Place	Summary of Events and Information	Remarks and references to Appendices
TIDWORTH, ENGLAND 14.12.15 4-30 a.m.	Left TIDWORTH STA. at 4-30 a.m. arriving FOLKESTONE 8-40 a.m. Left FOLKESTONE 9-30 a.m. The trooper was accompanied by a destroyer. Battalion embarked 1024 strong all ranks. Arrived CALAIS, FRANCE 12-55 p.m. Left CALAIS STA. 3 p.m. arriving BOULOGNE STA. 5-45 p.m. Marched to Rest Camp BOULOGNE arriving 7 p.m. The Transport and an advanced Party consisting of 3 Officers and 124 other ranks had left ENGLAND on 12th Nov 1915, for HAVRE. H.W.I.	
BOULOGNE, FRANCE 5-45 p.m.		
BOULOGNE. 15.12.15	General Routine Work Boulogne Rest Camp. A short route march was carried out at 2 p.m. in the afternoon. H.W.I.	
THIENNES. 16.12.15	Left BOULOGNE via PONT A BRIQUES at 10 a.m. where we picked up the Transport and Advanced Party from HAVRE, less one Officer who had been left at HAVRE for entraining duties. The train arrived STEENBECQUE at 6-10 p.m. we marched to THIENNES, arriving there 7-30 p.m. Billeted by 9-45 p.m. Very long village and first time billeting in dark, made it a lengthy task. H.W.I.	
THIENNES. 17.12.15	General Routine Work in billets. Distant firing heard. H.W.I.	
THIENNES. 18.12.15	General Routine Work in billets and preparation for move. H.W.I.	
LA MIQUELLERIE 19.12.15 near BUSNES.	Left THIENNES 8-25 a.m. arriving LA MIQUELLERIE 1 p.m. All billeted by 2 p.m. Routine Work. H.W.I.	
LA MIQUELLERIE 20.12.15 BETHUNE 20.12.15 1-30 p.m.	Second in Command, O.C. Coys, Bombing Officer and M-G Officer with parties of 4 NCOs per Coy. Start 6 a.m. to visit TRENCHES, GIVENCHY. Go in motor bus. Battalion left LA MIQUELLERIE 9-30 a.m. arriving BETHUNE 1-30 p.m. All billeted 3 p.m. Routine work in afternoon. H.W.I.	

WAR DIARY
or
INTELLIGENCE SUMMARY.
(Erase heading not required.)

Army Form C. 2118.

Instructions regarding War Diaries and Intelligence Summaries are contained in F.S. Regs., Part II. and the Staff Manual respectively. Title pages will be prepared in manuscript.

Hour, Date, Place	Summary of Events and Information	Remarks and references to Appendices
BETHUNE 21-12-15	BHQ and Nos 3 & 4 Coys remain BETHUNE. Nos 1 & 2 Coys proceed to TRENCHES, arriving WINDY CORNER, GIVENCHY 10 a.m. and relieving outgoing Bns by 1 p.m. Nos 1 & 2 Coys go for 24 hours. Routine work carried out issued in billets.	
BETHUNE 22-12-15	Nos 3 & 4 Coys arrive WINDY CORNER, GIVENCHY 10 a.m. and relieve Nos 1 & 2 Coys in the trenches. Nos 1 & 2 Coys return BETHUNE 3 p.m. Nos 3 & 4 Coys go for 24 hours. 1 Casualty No 1 Coy, wounded (self inflicted).	
BETHUNE 23-12-15	Nos 1 & 2 Coys relieve Nos 3 & 4 Coys in trenches and remain there 48 hours. Nos 3 & 4 Coys return 4 p.m. Casualty. 1 man (wounded).	
BETHUNE 24-12-15	Nos 3 & 4 Coys cleaning up and routine work. Casualties. 2 men (wounded).	
BETHUNE 25-12-15 HINGES 8 p.m.	Nos 3 & 4 Coys relieved Nos 1 & 2 in the trenches. Relief commenced 11 a.m. terminating 2 p.m. Nos 1 & 2 Coys then marched to HINGES to join Hd Qrs and Headquarters which was given 1½ hours notice to leave BETHUNE and billet in HINGES. The move was completed by 8 p.m. Delay was caused by the difficulty in obtaining transport.	
HINGETTE and AVELETTE 26-12-15	Bn moved from HINGES to HINGETTE and AVELETTE neighbouring villages. The move was commenced and completed early. Routine work.	
HINGETTE and AVELETTE 27-12-15	Nos 3 & 4 Coys arrived AVELETTE 3-15 p.m. from trenches, where they had been 48 hours. Each Coy had thus been 3 days in the trenches all told and during that time had been affiliated to Coys of Regular and Territorial Bns which had had experience of the trenches. The	

WAR DIARY
or
INTELLIGENCE SUMMARY.
(Erase heading not required.)

Army Form C. 2118.

Instructions regarding War Diaries and Intelligence Summaries are contained in F. S. Regs., Part II. and the Staff Manual respectively. Title pages will be prepared in manuscript.

Hour, Date, Place		Summary of Events and Information	Remarks and references to Appendices
Billets	HINGETTE & AVELETTE 27.12.15	Experience thus gained was extremely valuable and is likely to stand the Bn. in better than an if it had been put into the trenches at once and without some days from which to learn. For a newly arrived Bn. the test was a pretty severe one rather whole as there were frequent tours and long marches to be carried out. The spirit of all ranks is admirable. Casualties. 3 men (wounded) HWT	
Billets	" 28.12.15	Routine work in billets. HWT	
Billets	" 29.12.15	Routine Work in billets HWT	
Billets	ESSARS. 30.12.15	The Bn. marched from HINGETTE & AVELETTE to ESSARS arriving there about 2 p.m. Billeting completed 3 p.m. Routine Works carried out. HWT	

19th Battalion

ROYAL FUSILIERS

JANUARY 1916

98th Brigade.
33rd Division.

Confidential

WAR DIARY
or
INTELLIGENCE SUMMARY.
(Erase heading not required.)

Army Form C. 2118.

Instructions regarding War Diaries and Intelligence Summaries are contained in F.S. Regs., Part II. and the Staff Manual respectively. Title pages will be prepared in manuscript.

Hour, Date, Place	Summary of Events and Information	Remarks and references to Appendices
1.1.16. BRICKSTACKS Sub-Section A1	Very Quiet. The Germans did practically nothing. The Artillery Observation Officer of our Supporting Battery stated that the GERMAN wire immediately N of the LA-BASSEE — BETHUNE had been cut, from its appearance and the fact of its being folded back, not by Artillery but probably by other means. The Brigade, Bns on right and left and all Coys were warned. Patrols however were sent out at night to ascertain whether the wire had been cut and they reported a gap of about 5 yds in the same place as indicated by Artillery. The wire had been cut by hand, and loose ends were found lying about. In anticipation of an attack the greatest vigilance was maintained. The night however passed off quietly, almost unusually quiet.	
2.1.16 " "	The lull of overnight was the precursor of a storm. This has been remarked more than once and in this respect the usual rule of the German appears to desert him. The enemy by means best-known to himself discovered a relief was being carried out today. Up went hostile 'planes and a heavy, but hardly an intensive bombardment of our front, support and third line was commenced approximately at 10-30, just when the relief was at a corner estaminet at the junction of HARLEY STREET and the main LA BASSEE-BETHUNE ROAD are probably spies. They have every opportunity of gathering useful knowledge, and in an unobtrusive way take a great deal of interest in our movements. At about 11-30 when the relief was at its height the bombardment was at its intensest. 5.9" were sent on and across the main road, particular attention being paid to Bde Hd Qrs. The placing of and the rapidity with which the 5.9" came, appeared very like a barrage. Simultaneously our front & support line, particularly CUINCHY SUPPORT were heavily shelled with field guns and 4.2". At approximately 11.15 a.m a small mine was sprung in on left opposite the right Coy of the A & S Highlanders and at 11-30 a.m. a larger mine opposite our left front Coy (No 4). A fair amount of the parapet was blown in and our casualties were nearly all in this Coy. Total Casualties 2nd Lt WOOD killed. CAPT SHIPSTER (O.C. No 4 Coy) wounded, and of O.R. 8 killed and 18 wounded. No attack followed the springing of the mine or the heavy shelling, several Germans showed themselves very conspicuously over the parapet, but this was more bravado than intent to attack. The general situation on this day is	

WAR DIARY or INTELLIGENCE SUMMARY.

(Erase heading not required.)

Army Form C. 2118.

Instructions regarding War Diaries and Intelligence Summaries are contained in F.S. Regs., Part II. and the Staff Manual respectively. Title pages will be prepared in manuscript.

Hour, Date, Place	Summary of Events and Information	Remarks and references to Appendices
2.1.16. From Trenches (BRICKSTACKS) to Billets (BETHUNE)	is difficult to sum up. It suggests an intention to carry out an attack, but either something going wrong or a determination of the enemy to advance, frustrating the effort at the last moment. We were relieved by 16th K.R.R. The last platoon arrived BETHUNE about 3 p.m., by which time the billeting was completed. HWT	
3.1.16 Billets (BETHUNE)	The Battalion had billets at ECOLE DE JEUNES FILLES. The Billets were in a dirty condition when taken over, and much time was spent in cleaning them. H.Q. was at 65 ROE DE LILLE. HWT	
4.1.16 "	Routine Work. Rifle Range allotted us 9 Coy from 9 a.m to 12 noon.	
5.1.16 "	Routine Work. Warning received that BETHUNE might be shelled. Necessary action taken. All available cellars and dugouts rested. HWT	
6.1.16. BETHUNE) BEUVRY) HWT	~~No 2 Coy less 1 Pl, and No 3 Coy moved at 10 a.m. and billeted at BEUVRY with~~ ~~orders to go to~~ HWT Routine work. Rifle Range from 12 noon to 4 p.m. (allotted to No 1 Coy). HWT	
7.1.16. "	Routine work. Orders for move to trenches and hold ourselves in readiness. HWT	
8.1.16. BETHUNE) BEUVRY)	No 2 Coy less 1 Platoon and No 3 Coy, marched at 10 a.m and billeted at BEUVRY with orders to man MAISON ROUGE and KEEPS in Z.O Subsection at 9-30 a.m. 9.1.16. Owing to heavy shelling being anticipated the relief was carried out at 3-30 a.m. 9.1.16. No casualties. No 3 Coy occupied MAISON ROUGE, + BRANOO TRENCH, and LEWIS KEEP. 1 Platoon No 2 Coy SIMS KEEP, 1 pl RAILWAY KEEP. Owing to a mistake in the orders 1 Platoon No 2 Coy was sent back to ANNEQUIN SOUTH. HWT	

WAR DIARY or INTELLIGENCE SUMMARY.

Army Form C. 2118.

(Erase heading not required.)

Hour, Date, Place	Summary of Events and Information	Remarks and references to Appendices
9.1.16 Billets ANNEQUIN SOUTH	Hd Qrs, 1 Platoon No 2 Coy, No 1 Coy and No 4 Coy & Sapping Platoon vacated billets BETHUNE 8-20 am and marched to ANNEQUIN SOUTH. Billeting completed by 1pm. Billets exceptionally dirty. B[n] Hd Qrs at F.30.a.3½.8½. WWS	Reference Bethune Combined Sheet 1:40,000.
10.1.16 "	Supplied 2 Working Parties. We were shelled intermittently from 11 a.m. to 3 p.m. The shots were aimed at the Slag Heap mainly at L.5.b. Some of them going very near Bde HQ at L.5.b.5.7. Several shots were aimed at Anti Aircraft Battery at F.23.d, which was very conspicuously placed in open. Two hostile planes that had been circling over would have observed it as it was impossible not to see it. The guns however were entirely shifted, and apparently no damage done. All shells were 5.9" H.E. WWS	ditto.
11.1.16 "	Enemy dropped a few 5.9" H.E. again at Slag Heap. One of the shells fell on the road, smashing two motor lorries and killing one driver and three civilians, two of whom were children. Orders received that we were going to carry out an artillery bombardment from 7 pm to 7 a m (12.1.16) Routine work and improvement of billets. WWS	
12.1.16	Routine work. Supplied 5 fatigue parties. At 9 pm the enemy burst six shrapnel over the road. They all burst extremely high and did no damage. WWS	

WAR DIARY
or
INTELLIGENCE SUMMARY.
(Erase heading not required.)

Army Form C. 2118.

Instructions regarding War Diaries and Intelligence Summaries are contained in F.S. Regs., Part II. and the Staff Manual respectively. Title pages will be prepared in manuscript.

Hour, Date, Place	Summary of Events and Information	Remarks and references to Appendices
13.1.16 ANNEQUIN SOUTH	Routine Work. Very quiet day. Practically no shells, except the usual six light shrapnel at 9 p.m. HWT	
14.1.16 "	Routine Work and six shells at 9 p.m. HWT	
15.1.16. "	Routine work and preparation for move to trenches. Coy Commanders visit the line. HWT	
16.1.16. CAMBRIN TRENCHES.	Bn moved into CAMBRIN TRENCHES from SOUTH ANNEQUIN. Relief commenced at 4-30 p.m pm and was completed by 7-30 p.m. No shelling took place and there were no casualties. The Subsection taken over was "Z South" of Z.O, extending from left of MUD TRENCH on right to BOYAU 9. The enemy wire on the whole did not appear to be so substantial as in other parts of the line. It was mostly rusty but nevertheless afforded an efficient obstacle. The condition of "no-mans land" between the trenches is good, shell holes few and the ground flat, thus affording excellent ground over which to conduct an attack. The Trenches are in good condition on the whole. A portion of GUYS ALLEY, HAMILTON STREET (now renamed OLD BOOTS TRENCH) and RESERVE TRENCH are in bad condition. A working party of Pioneers Bn are to be put on this to clean and revet it. The Sapping Platoon are working on third line, improving the fire steps and building up parapet where broken down. This appears to be a very strong line, provided the third and subsequent rear lines are strengthened and wire improved. The front line wire was improved by the addition of numerous footballs. Nothing of importance noted. HWT	

(73989) W4141—463. 400,000. 9/14. H.&J. Ltd. Forms/C. 2118/10.

WAR DIARY or INTELLIGENCE SUMMARY.

(Erase heading not required.)

Army Form C. 2118.

Instructions regarding War Diaries and Intelligence Summaries are contained in F.S. Regs., Part II. and the Staff Manual respectively. Title pages will be prepared in manuscript.

Hour, Date, Place	Summary of Events and Information	Remarks and references to Appendices
17.1.16 TRENCHES	Enemy shelled SIMS KEEP and RAILWAY KEEP, front and support lines with whizz bangs and heavy shrapnel. No damage to our trenches. Three casualties all slight. No damage done to trenches. Our artillery retaliated effectively. One of our M.G. claims to have put enemy M.G. out of action. Snipers were very active today. The enemy did a considerable amount of work, but it was continually interrupted by our M.G. fire.	
18.1.16 "	Work done. Clearing bad or impassable trenches, connecting third line into fire trenches, augmenting wire by the putting up of rows of concertina into footballs in between. A new M.G. position and emplacement was made which enfiladed AVENY ALLEY. An albatross machine was sighted. It circled round our lines for about half an hour. It went away on the approach of four of our monoplanes.	HWS
19.1.16 "	A mine was sprung at 1.20am on the left, some distance away, another at 10.30p.m. Nothing unusual happened and it was not ascertained whether the mines were ours or enemy's.	HWS
20.1.16 "	Nothing unusual to report except a most unusual inactivity on the part of the enemy. No working parties were observed, no Very lights were sent up and the most complete silence prevailed.	
21.1.16 "	This unusual activity, evidently the precursor of organized work, was followed by much activity in the way of work on the part of the enemy. So tenacious were the enemy in continuing work that one working party which was fired on by heavy M.G. fire lay flat whilst the firing was going on and then resumed work immediately the firing ceased. This was repeated on five separate occasions.	

WAR DIARY
or
INTELLIGENCE SUMMARY.
(Erase heading not required.)

Army Form C. 2118.

Instructions regarding War Diaries and Intelligence Summaries are contained in F.S. Regs., Part II. and the Staff Manual respectively. Title pages will be prepared in manuscript.

Hour, Date, Place	Summary of Events and Information	Remarks and references to Appendices
21.1.16. TRENCHES	Even at 10-30 a.m. Enemy were noticed throwing earth up. That ceased when the artillery were turned on. New saps were noticed to the number of 7 Opposite our front. HWI	
22.1.16 "	It was noticed that the enemy were engaged during night in strengthening wire opposite their sap heads. The condition of the wire of our front and support line considerably improved. Quiet day. Little shelling or rifle fire. HWI	
23.1.16 "	Between 12 noon and 12-30 pm the Howitzers (4.5") were turned onto the new saps. Most of the shots fell into the enemy's trench or front line parapet, which was considerably damaged and most of the wire blown away. The saps were touched but seldom. 15 shots were "blinds" out of 50 fired. Situation otherwise normal. HWI	
24.1.16 " and BETHUNE (BILLETS)	Enemy artillery HWI was active. Our field guns bombarded the enemy's front trenches and the howitzers bombarded the communication trenches. Situation otherwise normal HWI. The enemy in retaliation for this and the pounding they had received the previous day proceeded to bombard our support and communication trenches with 4.2 (Shrapnel + HE) and field guns. The Battalion was relieved by 16th K.R.R. The relief commenced at 4-30 pm and was completed by 9 pm. Every platoon having marched independently from trenches to billets. Billeted at ECOLE MICHELET. There were two casualties, one man killed one man wounded	

WAR DIARY
or
INTELLIGENCE SUMMARY

(Erase heading not required.)

Army Form C. 2118

Instructions regarding War Diaries and Intelligence Summaries are contained in F. S. Regs., Part II. and the Staff Manual respectively. Title Pages will be prepared in manuscript.

Place	Date	Hour	Summary of Events and Information	Remarks and references to Appendices
BETHUNE (Billets)	24.2.16		Fortunately the enemy stopped shelling by 4 p.m, so the relief was completed without any casualties. HWI	
BILLETS BETHUNE	25/2/16		Battalion had baths at ECOLE DE JEUNES FILLES. Routine work. HWI	
BILLETS BETHUNE to ANNEQUIN FOSSE	26/2/16		Orders were received in preparation of the Kaiser's birthday to move up and be ready to reinforce. Orders to move to ANNEQUIN FOSSE were received at 9-49p.m. The Battalion moved off 9-57 pm and arrived ANNEQUIN FOSSE 11-15p.m. Bn H d Qrs at L.5.b.5.7 which were the HQ of the 100th Bde. The Bn now came under the orders of 100th Bde. HWI	
ANNEQUIN FOSSE	27/2/16		Kaiser's birthday and a quiet one at that. Routine Work. HWI	
"	28/2/16		Throughout the morning the village at the FOSSE was continuously shelled by the Germans who were evidently trying to find a battery which was just in front of the FOSSE. The shelling was continued in the afternoon. The shells were small and large shrapnel and H.E and a few 5.9". Two men were killed and 5 injured by a shrapnel which burst just outside the billet in which the men were. About 50 shells were sent by the Germans into BEUVRY. They were mostly 5.9" and a few 8.2". HWI	
from ANNEQUIN FOSSE to TRENCHES (BRICKSTACKS)	29/2/16		The day was quiet on the whole and at 4-30p.m. the Bn vacated billets and moved to Trenches (BRICKSTACKS) between CAMBRIN and CUINCHY (subsection A.1.). The relief was carried out without casualties and was completed by 7p.m. The Battalion relieved was the 20th R.F. HWI	

WAR DIARY or INTELLIGENCE SUMMARY.

Army Form C. 2118.

(Erase heading not required.)

Hour, Date, Place	Summary of Events and Information	Remarks and references to Appendices
30.1.16. TRENCHES. BRICKSTACKS.	Very misty overnight and during day. Very quiet in consequence. The trenches were in good condition but a considerable amount of work is required to bring them into really fine fettle to withstand attack. Considerable amount of wire, foot balls, sawstakes and concertina were put out. As far as could be ascertained the enemy had not touched their wire since the last month when we were in this subsection. The mine that was blown up on the 2nd Jan 1915 formed an enormous crater on the left of this subsection. The Eastern lip of the crater being about 5 yds behind our front line. The dimensions of the crater were roughly 50 feet deep and about 50 yards across. HWT	
31.1.16 " "	Work continued where necessary. Our Howitzers put a few shells into the German Support line, but nearly all the shells were "blinds". Artillery not active on either side. In the field 31.1.16 H W Smith Major & Adjt 19th Royal Fusiliers	

W W Gordon Lt Col
Cmdg. 19th Royal Fusiliers

98th Brigade
33rd Division

BATTALION CAME UNDER G.H.Q. 27.2.16.

19th BATTALION

ROYAL FUSILIERS

FEBRUARY 1916

WAR DIARY or INTELLIGENCE SUMMARY

(Erase heading not required.)

Army Form C. 2118

Place	Date	Hour	Summary of Events and Information	Remarks and references to Appendices
Subsection A1 CUINCHY	1/2/16		The enemy shelled our front line, support and communication trenches for one hour from 2-45 p.m. to 3-45 p.m. No casualties or damage from shell fire. Quiet day otherwise. HWT	
"	2.2.16		Nos 2 and 3 Coys relieved No 4 Coy and No 1 Coy in the firing line. The relief was commenced at 2pm and completed by 6 p.m. One man wounded. HWT	
"	3.2.16		Germans fired some shells mostly 4.2" with a few 5.9" into ANNEQUIN and along main LA-BASSEE ROAD. The day otherwise was uneventful. HWT	
"	4.2.16		Weather dull and wet after a considerable spell of fine and clear days. The Germans were very active with their grenades and minenwerfers, both large and small. Three casualties. HWT	
"	5.2.16		Quiet day. A few shells were dropped along the LA BASSEE ROAD soon after dusk, just at the time rations were being brought up. No damage was done. HWT	
"	6.2.16		Our artillery was particularly active during the day. Some shells fell short. A Test Gas Alarm was arranged. The message came at 11 p.m., was circulated to Coys by 11.5 p.m. and helmets were put, men in battle positions, and all anti gas apparatus in order by 11.20 p.m. Owing to not being able to use gas gongs etc the alarm took a longer time to circulate. It was found very difficult to see through the mica of the goggles and the glass of the tube helmets, and it is doubtful whether in the event of a real alarm there would be time for both. HWT	
"	7.2.16		Reinforcement in the shape of a draft of 20 men arrived. The day was quiet and uneventful. HWT	

WAR DIARY or INTELLIGENCE SUMMARY

Army Form C. 2118

Place	Date	Hour	Summary of Events and Information	Remarks and references to Appendices
SUB-SECTION A.1 CUINCHY	8.2.16	3pm	Two enemy aeroplanes passed over lines going West. The Germans shelled BRADDELS POINT and WOBURN ABBEY pretty freely. No damage. HWT	
"	9.2.16		Being a very bright day the Germans sent their 'planes over, but the object with which they had been apparently sent over, i.e. to locate our 15" guns was not successful. A Vickers Fighter engaged an Aviatik and another machine. Owing to its not being able to manoeuvre as fast as the German planes it was beaten off though it put up a very good fight. Our 15" guns shelled VERMELLES. Judging by appearances pretty effectively. HWT	!
"	10.2.16		One Coy of the 7th LEINSTERS attached for instruction. Though never in the trenches before they did very well. Quiet uneventful day. HWT	
"	11.2.16		A very quiet day. HWT	
"	12.2.16		There was a certain liveliness on the part of our artillery. From 1-30 pm to 5 p.m. we shelled the Boche with field guns, 4.5" and 9". The latter were directed at the BRICKSTACKS. HWT	
"	13.2.16		The enemy retaliated at precisely the same hour today. They commenced at 1-30 pm and ended at 5 p.m. They sent over all sizes of minnen-werfers, shrapnel and heavy stuff further back. They devoted a certain amount of attention to BnHQ but no shell came closer than 40 yards. Casualties. A billet next to Bn Hd Qrs was rendered untenable HWT	

WAR DIARY or INTELLIGENCE SUMMARY

Army Form C. 2118

(Erase heading not required.)

Place	Date	Hour	Summary of Events and Information	Remarks and references to Appendices
CUINCY BETHUNE	13.2.16		The Bn was relieved by the 1st Queens, and marched to BETHUNE. The relief was completed by 7-40 p.m. and every man billeted (MONTMERENCY BKS, BETHUNE) by 10 p.m. HWT	
BETHUNE	14.2.16		Routine work cleaning up. Much of the latter required after the long spell in the trenches, also MONTMERENCY BKS not too clean. HWT	
"	15.2.16		Leave to England commenced. HWT	
"	16.2.16		The Battalion had baths at the École du Jeunes Filles. HWT	
"	17.2.16		Routine work. HWT	
"	18.2.16		Routine work. HWT	
"	19.2.16		Routine work. We were visited by Boche planes which dropped 5 bombs at 10 p.m. Some telephone wires were damaged but no men hurt. HWT	
"	20.2.16		Routine work. HWT	
SUBSECTION Z1	21.2.16		The Bn relieved the 2nd R.W.F. in the trenches (subsection Z1). The relief was completed by 7-45 p.m. without incident. Wind East. HWT	
"	22.2.16		A quiet day. The advent of snow and cold winds made the snipers of both sides un-enterprising. HWT	
"	23.2.16		More snow and prevailing quiet men. HWT	

WAR DIARY
or
INTELLIGENCE SUMMARY
(Erase heading not required.)

Army Form C. 2118

Instructions regarding War Diaries and Intelligence Summaries are contained in F. S. Regs., Part II. and the Staff Manual respectively. Title Pages will be prepared in manuscript.

Place	Date	Hour	Summary of Events and Information	Remarks and references to Appendices
Subsection Z1	24/2/16		Wind NNE. Cold and quiet. HWT	
"	25/2/16		The Germans sent over some heavy "Minnies". One casualty from sniper. HWT	
"	26.2.16		The Bn was relieved in the trenches by the 2nd A & S Highlanders. The relief was completed by 4-55 pm. The Bn was billeted the night at ANNEQUIN SOUTH	
"	27.2.16		The fate we have some time anticipated has now overtaken us, i.e. being turned into an O.T.C. The Bn left ANNEQUIN SOUTH at 9-45 am and left BETHUNE by the 1-20pm train, for RACQUINGHEM. The Bn detrained at STOMER and arrived at RACQUINGHEM at 7-15pm. Billeting was completed by 9pm. HWT	
"	28.2.16		The Bn now having left the 33rd Divisional Area comes under the orders of GHQ Troops, STOMER. HWT	
"	29.2.16		Routine work & cleaning up.	

HW White
Major & Adjt
& O.C. 19th RF

Came from 98th Brigade 33rd Division 27.2.16.

19th BATTALION

ROYAL FUSILIERS

MARCH 1916

G. H. Q. TROOPS

WAR DIARY or INTELLIGENCE SUMMARY

Army Form C. 2118

Place	Date	Hour	Summary of Events and Information	Remarks and references to Appendices
Racquinghem	1/3/16		Lists of names of men recommended for Commission made out for G.H.Q. The Commanding Officer inspected the Battⁿ	
"	2.3.16		The Battⁿ proceeded on a Route March to Aire.	
"	3.3.16		Coy training	
"	4 "		Kit inspection: Coy training	
"	5 "		Sunday.	
"	6 "		Proposed Route March cancelled owing to heavy fall of snow. Major Tuite takes over the Command of N° 3 Coy. Lt P. Ingleson appointed Adjutant	
"	7		Battⁿ Route March to Arques.	
"	8		The Battⁿ was inspected by Brigadier General L.A.M. Stopford Comm^{dg} G.H.Q Troops. The following were his remarks "You could not have a nicer Battⁿ & I would not have missed seeing them. They are very steady in the ranks & extremely well turned out."	

WAR DIARY or INTELLIGENCE SUMMARY

Army Form C. 2118

Instructions regarding War Diaries and Intelligence Summaries are contained in F. S. Regs., Part II. and the Staff Manual respectively. Title Pages will be prepared in manuscript.

(Erase heading not required.)

Place	Date	Hour	Summary of Events and Information	Remarks and references to Appendices
Racquingham	9-3-16		Routine work.	
"	10-3-16		Route March	
"	11-3-16		All Coys under Coy Arrangements	
"	12-3-16		Voluntary Church Services	
"	13-3-16		All Coys: Coy Arrangements	
"	14-3-16		Route March. The first batch of 50 men went to N° 6 Officer Cadet Batt" Balliol Coll: Oxford, to undergo training with a view to taking up Commissions. Lt Skey was Conducting Officer.	
	15-3-16		Routine Work. All Coys under Coy Arrangement	
	16-3-16		" " " " " "	
	17-3-16		Route March	
	18-3-16		All Coys Company Arrangements	
	19-3-16		Voluntary Church Services. The 2nd Batch of 50 men left to go to N° 3 Cadet Batt" Bristol University. They were the Cpls of the Batt". Conducting Officer Capt: Shipster.	

WAR DIARY
or
INTELLIGENCE SUMMARY

(Erase heading not required.)

Army Form C. 2118

Place	Date	Hour	Summary of Events and Information	Remarks and references to Appendices
Rockingham	20.3.16		Routine work under Coy arrangements. The 3rd Batch of 50 men left for Cadet Training at No 4 Cadet Batt 9 Alfred St Oxford. They were all Corporals. Conducting Officer Lt Wattle. Thirty two men promoted L/Cpls (unpaid)	
"	21.3.16		Route Marches under Coy arrangements. The fourth batch of 50 men left for the Cadet Training in England, proceeding to No 4 Cadet Batt? 9 Alfred St Oxford. Conducting Officer 2Lt J.C. Evelyn.	
	22.3.16		The fifth batch of fifty men left for No 2 Cadet Batt - Pembroke Coll: Cambridge. Conducting Officer 2 Lt De la Rue.	
	23.3.16		The sixth batch of fifty men left for Cadet training in England. The men - seventy this time - went to No 1 Cadet Batt? Denham Uxbridge. Conducting Officers Capt Helps. Lt & Quartermaster F. Paton.	
	24.3.16		Route March. — Lecture to new NCO's by Major Morris	
	25.3.16		All Coys Coy Arrangements. Training of New N.C.Os.	

WAR DIARY or INTELLIGENCE SUMMARY

Army Form C. 2118

Place	Date	Hour	Summary of Events and Information	Remarks and references to Appendices
Racquinghem	26.3.16		The Battn paraded at 9.30 for inspection by General Cadorna the Italian C-in-C., who expressed himself very pleased with the Battn	
"	27		Routine Work under Coy Arrangements	
"	28		Route March	
"	29		Routine work under Coy Arrangements.	
"	30		" " " " "	
"	31		Route March. Lectures to NCO's & men under training for NCO's by Major Munro. Lectures to Coys under Coy arrangements	

P. Ingleson
Lt & Adjt
for O.C. 19th Royal Fusiliers

19th BATTALION

THE ROYAL FUSILIERS

APRIL 1916

Army Troops

WAR DIARY or INTELLIGENCE SUMMARY
(Erase heading not required.)

G.H.Q.

Army Form C. 2118

19 R Fus

Vol 5

Place	Date	Hour	Summary of Events and Information	Remarks and references to Appendices
1.4.16 Raeguingham	1-4-16		Routine work under Coy arrangements. Administered by 1st Army instead of G.H.Q Troops	
"	2-4-16		Voluntary Church Services	
"	3-4-16		Routine work under coy arrangements	
"	4-4-16		Route March. Lectures to Coys. Coy arrangements. Lecture to NCO's by Major Munro	
"	5-4-16		Routine work under Coy arrangements	
"	6-4-16		Route March. Lectures to Coys by O.C. Coys. Lecture to NCO's by Major Munro	
"	7-4-16		Routine work under coy arrangements	
"	8-4-16		Voluntary Church Services	
"	9-4-16		Routine work under Coy arrangements. A further batch of 25 men proceeded for Cadet training to No. 8 Cadet Batt. Whittington Barracks, Lichfield	
"	10-4-16			
"	11-4-16		Kit inspection	
"	12-4-16		Routine work under Coy arrangements	
"	13-4-16		" " " " Another batch of 30 men proceeded for Cadet training to No. 5 Cadet Batt. Trinity Coll. Cambridge	
"	14-4-16		Route March	
"	15-4-16		Routine work under Coy arrangements	
"	16-4-16		Voluntary Church Services	
"	17-4-16		Routine work under Coy arrangements	
"	18-4-16		Route March	

WAR DIARY or INTELLIGENCE SUMMARY

Army Form C. 2118

Instructions regarding War Diaries and Intelligence Summaries are contained in F. S. Regs., Part II. and the Staff Manual respectively. Title Pages will be prepared in manuscript.

(Erase heading not required.)

Place	Date	Hour	Summary of Events and Information	Remarks and references to Appendices
Racquinghem	19-4-16		Routine work under Coy arrangements	
"	20-4-16		" " " " "	
"	21-4-16		Good Friday. Coy arrangements	
"	22-4-16		Routine work under Coy arrangements. The five newly joined Subalterns 2/Lts Scott, Roper, Wood, Wright-Ingle & Cooper, reported to 2nd Army at Bailleul for instruction in trench warfare.	
"	23-4-16		Easter Sunday. Voluntary Church Services. Information was received on the evening of this day that the Battn was going to be broken up the other two Fusilier Battns 18th & 21st were to share the same fate. Orders were received to proceed to ETAPLES for that purpose.	
"	24-4-16		Routine work under Coy arrangements.	
"	25-4-16		Routine work. A draft of 71 men & one officer Lt Palmer was posted to the Battn coming from ETAPLES, whither we are due to proceed tomorrow for disbandment.	
"	26-4-16		Departure of Battn to ETAPLES postponed till 27th. All the riding horses of the Battn were sent to the DDR 2nd Army in accordance with orders. Two new officers 2/Lts Clipton & Gillmore were posted to the Battn	
"	27-4-16		The Battn paraded at 7.15 a.m., entrained at WARDRECQUES & proceeded to the Base at ETAPLES, coming under orders from JAG 3rd Echelon & administered by Camp Commandant ETAPLES. ETAPLES was reached at 3.30 p.m.	

WAR DIARY or INTELLIGENCE SUMMARY

Army Form C. 2118

(Erase heading not required.)

Instructions regarding War Diaries and Intelligence Summaries are contained in F. S. Regs., Part II. and the Staff Manual respectively. Title Pages will be prepared in manuscript.

Place	Date	Hour	Summary of Events and Information	Remarks and references to Appendices
U Camp ETAPLES	28-4-16		The Battⁿ is in tents in U Camp ETAPLES. The Camp is situated among the sand-dunes about 2 miles from the sea. A Draft of 100 men was sent by the Batt: to 9th Battⁿ (12th I.B.D) situated in the same Camp. Time of departure 2 p.m.	
ETAPLES	29-4-16		Routine Work. General cleaning of lines.	
"	30-4-16		The following drafts were supplied by the Battⁿ:- 40 men to 12th R.F. 24th Div: Conducting Officer Lt Cottrell 30 " to 17th R.F 2nd Div: " " Lt Watts 30 " to 22nd R.F 2nd Div: " " Lt Long.	

P. Nylisson
Lt Adjt
19th Royal Fusiliers.

ARMY TROOPS
-++++++++++++-

DISBANDED 21st May 1916.

19th BATTALION

ROYAL FUSILIERS

M A Y 1 9 1 6

Disbands former [?]

Copy

WAR DIARY
or
INTELLIGENCE SUMMARY.
(Erase heading not required.)

19th R. Fus.

Army Form C. 2118.

Instructions regarding War Diaries and Intelligence Summaries are contained in F.S. Regs., Part II. and the Staff Manual respectively. Title pages will be prepared in manuscript.

Hour, Date, Place		Summary of Events and Information	Remarks and references to Appendices
ETAPLES	1.5.16	Routine work under company arrangements.	
	2.5.16	Do. Reveillé at 5.30 a.m. in future instead of 6.0. as hitherto.	
	3.5.16	Do. Special attention being paid to the training of men going for commissions. They are very keen, and voluntary parades and lectures are often well attended.	
	4.5.16	Routine work under coy. arrangements. LT. & ADJUTANT P. INGLESON } left for England to take up 2nd LIEUT. C. BARRINGTON BROWN } Staff appointments	2nd LT. B.J. HUBBARD appointed Acting Adjutant
	5.5.16	Routine work under coy arrangements A draft of 28 men proceeded to 23rd R.F. Conducting Officer. 2nd LT. E.W. GIBSON 22nd R.F.	
	6.5.16	Routine work 18 men of regimental transport, who had marched independently from RACQUINGHEM to ABBEVILLE rejoined the Bn.	
	7.5.16	Sunday. No church parade. Torrential rain A draft of 12 men in charge of the senior private left for 23rd R.F.	
	8.5.16	Routine work under company arrangements LT. P.B. COTTRELL left for England. 2nd LT. E STEVENSON joined the Bn.	
	9.5.16	Routine work.	
	10.5.16	The battalion band 21 strong under the Drum Major (Sgt. J.W. CASTREE) proceeded to the 33rd Division, 1st Army.	

Copy

WAR DIARY
or
INTELLIGENCE SUMMARY
(Erase heading not required.)

Army Form C. 2118

Instructions regarding War Diaries and Intelligence Summaries are contained in F.S. Regs., Part II. and the Staff Manual respectively. Title Pages will be prepared in manuscript.

Place	Date	Hour	Summary of Events and Information	Remarks and references to Appendices
ETAPLES	10.5.16 (cont'd)		The Batt'n handed over its lines to the 41st I.B.D. and moved to the 33rd I.B.D. Pte LAWSON left for England to take up commission in R.N.R.	
	11.5.16		Routine work under company arrangements. Kit inspection.	
	12.5.16		Do	
	13.5.16		Do	
	14.5.16		Voluntary church services as alternative to morning parade under coy arrangements	
	15.5.16		Routine work. In afternoon, parade for clothes washing. CAPT C.S. MEARES, 2/LT F.J. EATHORNE, 2/LT N. LAIDLAY were transferred to 24th Bn. RF and proceeded to join that Bn at the front.	
	16.5.16		Routine work. A party of 50 N.C.O.s and men proceeded to No 10 Officers cadet Bn GAILES. Conducting officer was 2/LT. STEIN.	
	17.5.16		Routine work. Major R.P.H. MONRO (2nd in command of Bn) proceeded to HQ 4th Army for instruction as A.P.M. Parties proceeded to England for cadet training as under:- 42 NCOs & men to OXFORD. Conducting officer from 18th RF CAPT. HELPS. 97 CAMBRIDGE. 135 BALLIOL, OXFORD. from 21st RF	as A.P.M.

WAR DIARY
or
INTELLIGENCE SUMMARY
(Erase heading not required.)

Army Form C. 2118

Instructions regarding War Diaries and Intelligence Summaries are contained in F. S. Regs., Part II. and the Staff Manual respectively. Title Pages will be prepared in manuscript.

Place	Date	Hour	Summary of Events and Information	Remarks and references to Appendices
ETAPLES	18.5.16	(cont'd)	Major H.N. TUITE } 2/Lt. R.C. LONG } proceeded to No 11 Officers Cadet Bn. CAMBERLEY as Instructors.	
"	19.5.16		The total strength of Bn is now 49, of whom all but three are P.B. or Employed men	
	20.5.16		Lt C H WATTS } attached to 35th I.B.D. } J H PALMER } 20th I.B.D. } for temporary duty.	
	21.5.16		10 P.B. men transferred to 20th R.F. The Commanding Officer leaves for England 23.5.16; the Adjutant 22.5.16. The Battalion must therefore now be considered to be disbanded.

B.J. Hubbard
2/Lt. and Adjutant
19th Bn. Royal Fusiliers | |

C O P Y.
———————

1.

Officer, i/c Records,
Royal Fusiliers,
H O U N S L O W.

Will you please forward to this Office, a copy of the Duplicate War Diary of the 19th. Bn.Royal Fusiliers, for the months of September, and October, 1916.

It is not possible to obtain these copies from the Battalion as it is now disbanded.

(Sgnd.) M.Yates, Captain
D. A. A. G.

G.H.Qrs.
3rd. Echelon.
11/2/1917.

==

2.

TO:- THE SECRETARY,
WAR OFFICE.

With reference to Min. 1., no copies of "War Diary" of the 19th. R.Fusiliers have been received in this Office.

Will you please inform me if 2 copies were received by you.

Infy. Record Office. H'slow.
Ref. No. R.F.1364/2.

(Sgnd.) A.L.Armstrong? 2/Lt.for Col.
i/c Infantry Records, Hounslow

16/2/17.

==

3.

D. A. A. G.
3rd. Echelon.

Reference minute 1, no War Diaries of the 19th. Bn., Royal Fusiliers for the months of September and October, 1916, have been received in the War Office. It is understood that this Bn. had practically all its men receive Commissions in the Summer of 1916, and it is thought to be doubtful whether diaries exist for September and October.

(Sgnd.) B.Grindle.

War Office.
C.2.

2nd. March, 1917.

==

C O P Y.

TO :- Capt. Atkinson.

Are these Diaries with you, please?

(Sgnd.) H.G.Hobson,
Registry Room, 407.
War Office.

21/2/17.
=*

No diary has been received from the 19th. Royal Fusiliers of a later date than May, 1916.

28/2/1917.

(Sgnd.) C.T.Atkinson, Capt.,
Hist. Section. C.I.D.

=*

I presume the Battn. was in France on the dates mentioned?

(Sgnd.) W.W.Harris. R. 23/2.

=*

R.
(thro' S.D.2.)

Whether this unit as such was in France during the months mentioned we cannot say. It went to France as a part of 98th. Infy. Bde. (33rd. Divn.) about 12/15th Nov. 1915.

(Sgnd.) J.C.Chambers, Capt.,
D.A.A.G.

M.
26/2/17.
=*

R.
(thro' A.G.)

This Unit formed pary of the Public School (98th.) Brigade, and was taken out of the 33rd. Div., in which Divn. I was serving, during the early Summer of 1916.

I dont know whether it was disbanded by September but should think it very probable as practically all its members were given Commissions. I doubt therefore whether it has a War Diary for the months in question. M.F.Records should be able to say definitely when the Unit was disbanded.

(Sgnd.) A.Symons, Lt. Col.
G.S.

S.D./27/2/1.?

WO 95 2427/4

21 BN ROYAL FUSILIERS
1915 NOV - 1916 FEB

33 DIV
9x BDE

21 BATTN ROYAL FUS

1915 NOV — 1916 FEB

DISBANDED APRIL 1916

98th Brigade
33rd Division.

Battalion disembarked Calais 14.11.15.

21st BATTALION

ROYAL FUSILIERS

NOVEMBER 1 9 1 5.

WAR DIARY or ~~INTELLIGENCE SUMMARY~~.

(Erase heading not required.)

Army Form C. 2118.

Hour, Date, Place	Summary of Events and Information	Remarks and references to Appendices
8 a.m. Nov 14th 1915 PERHAM DOWN.	The Battalion*, strength 30 Officers and 994 Other Ranks, including attached, left No 3 Camp, PERHAM DOWN, en route for Active Service in FRANCE.	* Less 122 NCOs & men & 4 Officers (including 1st Line Transport) who left PERHAM DOWN 12.11.15, travelling via SOUTHAMPTON & HAVRE.
5 pm Nov 14th 1915 CALAIS	Arrived at CALAIS, via FOLKESTONE, per S.S. PRINCESS VICTORIA.	
8 pm. Nov 14th 1915 BOULOGNE	Arrived by train at BOULOGNE	
9.40 pm " "	" OSTROHOVE LARGE REST CAMP. Weather fine.	
Nov 15.	Remained at BOULOGNE. Nothing of any account took place. Weather fair.	
Night 15/16 Nov.	Heavy snowstorm: six inches of snow on Camp in morning 16th	
11.50 pm Nov 16 " 17	Marched from OSTROHOVE Camp. Entrained 3.55 am 17th at PONT DE BRIQUES, after long wait in rain. Transport joined Battn: on train, but 2 Officers & 66 O.R. of the advance party mentioned above, having been detained at SOUTHAMPTON, did not join up to day.	
9.50 am 17th Nov: 18th Nov THIENNES	Arrived THIENNES, where Battn was billeted by 1pm. Above mentioned 2 Officers and 66 O.R. joined up at about 8 a.m. One H.D. Mare, which strained itself during yesterday's journey died, and was buried.	THIENNES Ref: Sheet 36 a S.E. also HAZEBROUCK Sheet 5 a
8.45 am 19th Nov CANTRAINNES	Battn marched from THIENNES arriving at CANTRAINNES at 2 pm. where they were billeted by 3.15 pm	CANTRAINNG Ref BETHUNE Combined Sheet V. 7.

WAR DIARY or INTELLIGENCE SUMMARY

Army Form C. 2118.

Instructions regarding War Diaries and Intelligence Summaries are contained in F.S. Regs., Part II. and the Staff Manual respectively. Title pages will be prepared in manuscript.

(Erase heading not required.)

Hour, Date, Place	Summary of Events and Information (2nd i/c of each Company)	Remarks and references to Appendices
Nov. 20th CANTRAINNES	Major H.F FENN, 2nd i/c, & left at 7 a.m., to go by Motor-bus for trenches, rejoining Battn at BÉTHUNE in the evening.	CANTRAINNE Ref BETHUNE Combined Sheet V.7.
9.40 a.m.	The Battn marched from CANTRAINNES, arriving in BÉTHUNE at 1 p.m., where the men were billeted by 5 p.m. in a poor part of the town – AVENUE de BRUAY, near GARE DU NORD. The Battn was attached to 22nd Inf. Bde. for instruction. The Staff Capt of 22nd Bde called upon C.O. at 2 p.m.	
Nov. 21st BETHUNE and A SECTION TRENCHES	The C.O., the Adjutant, & 2 Platoons from each Coy, under O.C. Coys, proceeded to trenches immediately SOUTH of LA BASSÉE CANAL for 24 hrs instruction. Nos 1 and 2 Coys were attached to the 1st STAFFORDS, in SUBSECTION A1, & Nos 3 & 4 to 2nd R. WARWICKS in A.2. The C.O. returned in the evening to BETHUNE.	BETHUNE Ref BETHUNE Combined Sheet E. 10 and 11.
Nov. 22nd BEUVRY and A SECTION TRENCHES	On 22nd/11/15, 22nd Bde was relieved by 5th Bde, & the attachment of the Battalion for instruction was transferred to 5th Bde from 22nd. The Platoons attached to the STAFFORDS & WARWICKS in the trenches were relieved by other platoons of the Bn when those Regiments were relieved by the 1st Queens and 2nd H.L.I. respectively. The relieved Platoons moved out to Billets at BEUVRY, whither remainder of Battn also moved during the morning.	BEUVRY Ref BETHUNE Combined Sheet F. 14.
Nov. 23rd BEUVRY and A SECTION TRENCHES	The 23rd was spent in cleaning up clothing and Equipment by those platoons not in trenches. Of these latter, 2 casualties occurred today, 1 man killed, & 1 wounded.	

WAR DIARY or INTELLIGENCE SUMMARY.

Army Form C. 2118.

Instructions regarding War Diaries and Intelligence Summaries are contained in F.S. Regs., Part II. and the Staff Manual respectively. Title pages will be prepared in manuscript.

(Erase heading not required.)

Hour, Date, Place	Summary of Events and Information	Remarks and references to Appendices
Nov. 23rd 1915 BEUVRY and A SECTION TRENCHES	The Battn Signallers and Machine Gun Section proceeded to trenches today, the latter under Brigade arrangements. The platoons in trenches were relieved today.	BEUVRY Ref BETHUNE Combined Sheet F.14.
Nov. 24th 1915 BEUVRY and A SECTION TRENCHES	A working party˟ under command of Major H.F. FENN proceeded to trenches to carry out repairs and improvements. Of these 2 men were wounded and 3 killed by a German Rifle Grenade which burst in the trench where the group was working. The remainder of Battn at BEUVRY were instructed in use of gas helmets, and in care of feet in trenches, and in measures to be taken in case of gas attack.	˟50 Men & 1 Officer per Coy
Nov. 25th BEUVRY and A SECTION TRENCHES	A working party, similar to that sent yesterday, but drawn from other platoons, under command of Major P.E. STANLEY proceeded to A Section trenches this morning, leaving BEUVRY at 7.30 a.m. Those who formed the working party yesterday, were given the instruction in gas, etc. which they missed yesterday.	
Nov. 26th ANNEQUIN NORTH. And A SECTION B1 SUBSECTION } TRENCHES	The Battn left BEUVRY at 11 a.m. for ANNEQUIN NORTH arriving there at 12. noon. Weather - very cold and hail, rain & sleet falling abundantly. No 1 Coy, attached to 1st QUEENS and No 3 Coy, attached to 2nd WORCESTERS proceeded to A1 & B1 Subsections respectively, for Company training in the trenches. Attachments to end at 10 a.m. tomorrow	ANNEQUIN N. Ref BETHUNE Combined Sheet F.23.

WAR DIARY
or
INTELLIGENCE SUMMARY.

(Erase heading not required.)

Army Form C. 2118.

Instructions regarding War Diaries and Intelligence Summaries are contained in F. S. Regs., Part II. and the Staff Manual respectively. Title pages will be prepared in manuscript.

Hour, Date, Place	Summary of Events and Information	Remarks and references to Appendices
Nov. 27th 1915 ANNEQUIN NORTH and A1 Subsections B1 " TRENCHES	Nos 2 & 4 Coys relieved Nos 1 & 4 Coys respectively in the trenches, being attached to QUEENS & WORCESTERS as yesterday. One man of No 2 Coy was wounded. These Coys will rejoin the Battn. tomorrow.	ANNEQUIN N. Ref: BETHUNE Combined Sheet F. 23.
Nov. 28th 1915. BETHUNE.	The Battn. moved from ANNEQUIN N. to BETHUNE. Starting at 8 a.m. On arrival in the latter town at 10 a.m. the Battn: was billeted in the COLLEGE DE JEUNES FILLES. The two Coys coming out from the trenches marched in to BETHUNE independently, arriving in time for the midday meal.	BETHUNE Ref: BETHUNE Combined Sheet E. 10 & 11.
Nov. 29th 1915 LES HARISOIRS	The Battn. moved from BETHUNE at 9.30 a.m. for LES HARISOIRS. Much delay was caused in getting into BILLETS at the latter place, as the accommodation was quite insufficient. However by the kindness of the O.C. 2nd A. & S. Highlanders all men were comfortably billeted during the afternoon. The 2nd A.&S.H. were billeted at MONT BERNENCHON, which village adjoins that of LES HARISOIRS.	LES HARISOIRS Ref: BETHUNE Combined Sheet V. 2 a and b.
Nov. 30th 1915 LES HARISOIRS.	The day was spent in cleaning up equipment, clothing etc. Weather - wet with push wind. Nothing of importance to record today.	

21st BATTALION

ROYAL FUSILIERS

DECEMBER 1915

98th Brigade.
33rd Division.

WAR DIARY or INTELLIGENCE SUMMARY.

(Erase heading not required.)

Army Form C. 2118.

Hour, Date, Place	Summary of Events and Information	Remarks and references to Appendices
December 1st 1915 LES HARISOIRS.	The day was spent in various parades under Company arrangements, & in practice in throwing live bombs. Weather improving. Nothing of consequence to record.	LES HARISOIRS Ref BETHUNE Combined Sheet V.2.a. and b.
Dec: 2nd 1915 LES HARISOIRS EPINETTE & FESTUBERT.	The Battn: marched out from LES HARISOIRS at 12.45 pm arriving in billets on the "VILLAGE LINE", EPINETTE & FESTUBERT at 5.30 pm.; of the other Bns: of the 98th Bde. the 19th RF, on the RIGHT, and the 1st MX, on the left, manned the trenches, while the 2nd A. & S.H. were in reserve at LE TOURET. Our Bn: Depôt, with 1st Line Transport was placed at LOISNE, where also Bde: Hqrs: have been taken up. The disposition of the Bn: was Nos: 1, 2 & 4 Coys in EPINETTE, & No: 3 Coy: in FESTUBERT, this latter Coy finding garrisons for FESTUBERT CENTRAL & EAST KEEPS, & also for KEEPS at TUNING FORK E., ROUTE A, and LOISNE E.	EPINETTE Ref BETHUNE Combined Sheet X.18.C. & 24a. FESTUBERT Ref BETHUNE Combined Sheet X.25.d. TUNING FORK E. Ref: BETHUNE Combined Sheet X.29.d.10.2. ROUTE A. KEEP. Ref BETHUNE Combined Sheet X.29.6.6½.7. LOISNE E. KEEP Ref. BETHUNE Combined Sheet X.28.a.9.7.
Dec: 3rd 1915 EPINETTE & FESTUBERT.	The day was spent in cleaning up the billets, making such improvements as were possible, & endeavouring to make some of the billets more or less shell-proof. No men are allowed to leave their billets without the permission of an Officer, & those who must do so, have to move in small bodies. A working party was sent to work under R.E. supervision in the Southern Subsection, occupied by 19th RF. This party reported to R.E. Officer at FESTUBERT CHURCH at 4.30 pm. On their return 3 casualties (3 men wounded) were reported.	
Dec: 4th 1915 EPINETTE & FESTUBERT	The Day was spent in further improving billets. Those men who were on last night's working party were off duty for the forenoon. Another working party — same time & place was supplied today. No casualties. Weather cold & showery.	

WAR DIARY or INTELLIGENCE SUMMARY

Army Form C. 2118.

(Erase heading not required.)

Hour, Date, Place	Summary of Events and Information	Remarks and references to Appendices
Dec: 5th 1915. FESTUBERT & EPINETTE	Working parties were supplied as for the last two days. Nothing worth reporting has happened, except that about a dozen shrapnel have fallen around EPINETTE, mostly near No 4 Coy's billet — no damage was done. The Germans were evidently after some of our 18 pounders, which were situate immediately behind No 4's billet.	
Dec: 6th 1915. FESTUBERT & EPINETTE. & SOUTHERN SUBSECTn TRENCHES.	The Battn relieved the 19th R.F. in SOUTHERN Subsection — reliefs commencing at 4.30 pm, except the M.G. Section, which has two guns in FESTUBERT CENTRAL, & 2 in FESTUBERT EAST KEEP. These guns are to remain in their present position. No 1 Coy relieved the left of the firing line, No 3 Coy the right of firing line, No 4 Coy left of reserve line, & No 2 Coy right of reserve line. No 2 Coy also found garrison for GOLDTHEY'S KEEP, while No 3 also occupied that part of the support line on the right which is considered tenable. All the trenches are in a deplorable condition. BARNTON RD — the main communication trench is only usable as far as the OLD BRITISH LINE (reserve line) — & the front line is divided into various small "islands" — each inaccessible from the other except by night — when the method employed is to go over the parapet. Relieving is of course only possible by night, & has to be done overland, the trenches being in many cases five feet deep in water. The weather is wet, which does not tend to make matters any easier. The relief was completed by 9 p.m. without casualty. Prior to relief. O.R.S. R.C.O. Sgt. T.L.W. STROTHER was wounded by shell in FESTUBERT EAST KEEP.	

WAR DIARY
~~INTELLIGENCE SUMMARY~~.
(Erase heading not required.)

Army Form C. 2118.

Instructions regarding War Diaries and Intelligence Summaries are contained in F. S. Regs., Part II. and the Staff Manual respectively. Title pages will be prepared in manuscript.

Hour, Date, Place	Summary of Events and Information	Remarks and references to Appendices
Dec: 7th 1915 SOUTHERN SUBSECTN TRENCHES. FESTUBERT.	Nothing of importance has occurred today; the weather remains wet and cold. The Signallers have been busy laying new wires, & joining up GORDNEY'S KEEP, which has not previously been connected by 'phone. It is hoped that by tomorrow the two front line Coys, the right support, the right reserve, & GORDNEY'S will all be in permanent telephonic connection with Hqrs – new D.5. cable being laid throughout.	
Dec: 8th 1915 DITTO.	Telephone communication above referred to has now been definitely established. No: 1 Coy have, by G.O.C's orders, been thinned out in front line, & half the Coy: gone into billets in the VILLAGE LINE at FESTUBERT. No 2 & half of No 4 Coys are relieving No 3 & half of No 1 Coys in the front line at 7.30pm tonight. One man was reported as accidentally wounded yesterday 7th in No 1 Coy. This is Pte Harris No who was wounded by Pte Metcalfe No while the latter was cleaning his rifle. Disciplinary action is being held over until the Battn leaves the Trenches for period of Rest.	
Dec: 9th 1915 Ditto.	Nothing of consequence to record; enemy very quiet, apart from occasional desultory shelling of FESTUBERT. Relief carried out without casualty. Weather continues wet and gusty.	

WAR DIARY or INTELLIGENCE SUMMARY.

(Erase heading not required.)

Army Form C. 2118.

Instructions regarding War Diaries and Intelligence Summaries are contained in F.S. Regs., Part II. and the Staff Manual respectively. Title pages will be prepared in manuscript.

Hour, Date, Place	Summary of Events and Information	Remarks and references to Appendices
Dec: 10th 1915. SOUTHERN SUBSECTION TRENCHES – FESTUBERT.	Still quiet. What slight repairs and improvements are possible under existing weather conditions being carried out. The rationing arrangements we have adopted in this SUBSECTION & which appear to meet the case fairly satisfactorily are as follows: 1st line transport bring rations to railhead at ESTAMINET CORNER, where they are loaded on to trucks by a party from one of the reserve coys & run up the light railway to the OLD BRITISH LINE: here they are dumped, and guides from the various front line posts meet the ration parties supplied by the reserve coys, & conduct them to their destinations – the rations being made up at the Depot into quantities sufficient for these various posts, & packed in sandbags. Water is taken up in petrol cans. The rations arrive at ESTAMINET CORNER at 6 p.m. & are up at OLD BRITISH LINE by 8 p.m.	ESTAMINET CORNER Ref: BETHUNE Combined Sheet F.6.c.3.8.
Dec: 11th 1915 DITTO. + GORRE & LE HAMEL	Still quiet. One casualty (1 man wounded) was reported yesterday from CORONER'S KEEP. The C.O. and Coy Commanders of 7th R. Sussex Regt: who relieve us tonight came up to reconnoitre. It was decided between our C.O. & O.C. R. Sussex to abandon the support line on the right – as this has become hopelessly untenable. This was therefore done during the afternoon. The Battn: moved out when relieved to GORRE and LE HAMEL. 1 Casualty occurred – one man missing. This man took a party of 7th R. Sussex up to the front line – was seen to leave on his homeward journey, & has not been seen since. 1 H.D. horse of our 1st Line transport was also wounded by shrapnel in the back. Relief was reported complete by 11.40 p.m.	GORRE Ref: BETHUNE Combined Sheet F.3.C. LE HAMEL – X.20.C.
Dec: 12th 1915 GORRE & LE HAMEL + HINGETTE.	The Battn: left GORRE & LE HAMEL at noon for HINGETTE, being in billets at HINGETTE by 3 p.m. Weather showery: nothing to record.	HINGETTE Ref: BETHUNE Combined Sheet W.10, 11, & 17.

WAR DIARY
or
INTELLIGENCE SUMMARY.
(Erase heading not required.)

Army Form C. 2118.

Instructions regarding War Diaries and Intelligence Summaries are contained in F. S. Regs., Part II. and the Staff Manual respectively. Title pages will be prepared in manuscript.

Hour, Date, Place	Summary of Events and Information	Remarks and references to Appendices
Dec: 13th 1915 HINGETTE L'ECLEME – ROBECQ.	The Bn. left HINGETTE at 11:45 am for REST BILLETS at L'ECLEME. This district was reported by the billeting Officer Capt J.E. Musgrave late last night as inundated, & the Adjutant rode over to Bde Hqrs at GONNEHEM to see what was to be done under the circumstances. The G.O.C. instructed that if practicable these billets were to be occupied. This was found possible, although the men had to walk through a foot of water on the road to enter the billets. The billets, once entered, proved to be good, & the whole Battn: was in billets by 3 p.m. The weather was fair & Capt. Musgrave reported that the water was appreciably lower than on the previous day.	Billets between L'ECLEME & ROBECQ. (Bn Rest Billets) Ref: BETHUNE Combined Sheet P. 35. & V. 4. GONNEHEM. Ref: BETHUNE Combined Sheet V. 18. a. and c.
Dec: 14th 1915 L'ECLEME.	The day was spent in cleaning up – badly needed after the particularly filthy trenches recently occupied. Two Coys (No 1 & 2) had hot baths at Bde: Baths, GONNEHEM. The water on the road from L'ECLEME to ROBECQ has gone down very considerably in the night, & the whole length of the billet area can now be traversed without wading.	
Dec: 15th 1915 L'ECLEME.	Day spent in further cleaning up. The other two Coys (3 & 4) bathed at GONNEHEM. Weather dull & showery – but water still going down.	
Dec 16th 1915 L'ECLEME.	Day spent as follows: morning, Platoon and Arm Drill: afternoon cleaning up billets, & touching up Clothing equipment etc: for G.O.C's inspection tomorrow. The Adjutant inspected Companies on parade in the morning, & found that although the equipment generally was in good order, considerably more work would have to be done upon it before G.O.C.'s parade tomorrow.	

WAR DIARY
~~INTELLIGENCE SUMMARY~~
(Erase heading not required.)

Army Form C. 2118.

Instructions regarding War Diaries and Intelligence Summaries are contained in F.S. Regs., Part II. and the Staff Manual respectively. Title pages will be prepared in manuscript.

Hour, Date, Place	Summary of Events and Information	Remarks and references to Appendices
Dec 16th 1915 (ctd) L'ECLEME.	Various parties were sent hourly throughout the day to take instruction from R.E. in erecting wire entanglements, & also parties of machine gunners to practice the erection of hasty machine gun emplacements, also under R.E. supervision.	
Dec: 17th 1915. Do:	The Brigadier General commanding 98th Infantry Brigade (Bgdr. Gen. E.P. STRICKLAND) inspected the Battn: on parade at 11.45 am, & afterwards interviewed O.C. Companies at the Orderly Room. He expressed himself as dissatisfied with the condition of the leather equipment of the Battn:. The C.O. subsequently interviewed O.C. Coys in this connection.	
Dec: 18th 1915. Do:	At 5.30 a.m. orders were received from Brigade for the Battn: to pass ROAD JUNCTION V.28.a.9.3. at am: This was a test alarm, & the Battn: turned out & was on the road in plenty of time to take its place in Brigade column of route at the appointed time & place. The C.O. at a subsequent meeting of O.C. Coys expressed himself satisfied with the execution of the practice. Nothing further to record.	
Dec: 19th 1915. Do:	Sunday – no parades. Part of day spent in cleaning equipment. Nothing to record.	
Dec: 20th 1915. Do:	Morning spent in Platoon & Arm Drill, dummy bomb throwing, & lectures on bombing: M.G. Section – gun drill & lecture on M.G. tactics. The C.O. inspected the Bn. on parade at 2.30 p.m., & noted considerable improvement in the turn-out.	

WAR DIARY or INTELLIGENCE SUMMARY

Army Form C. 2118.

Hour, Date, Place	Summary of Events and Information	Remarks and references to Appendices
Dec. 21st 1915. L'ECLÈME	The Battalion attended a lecture & demonstration of the use of gas-helmets at V.6.C.7.4½ (Béthune combined Sheet). This was most interesting, & calculated to give all ranks confidence in these gas-helmets, as all had to pass through a chamber filled with gas, with their helmets on. The lecturer also emphasized the necessity of constantly inspecting these helmets. Nothing further to record — except that Major H.P.FENN & O.C. Coys attended a tactical lecture given by the Brigadier at the Cinema, GONNEHEM during the afternoon.	
Dec. 22nd 1915 Do.	The day was spent in small parades under Coy: arrangement for training. Nothing of note has occurred.	
Dec. 23rd 1915. Do.	A further visit today from G.O.C. 98th Bde., who inspected No. 1 & 4 Coys at training. Further parties from each Coy: attended wiring instruction under R.E., as described on 16th inst.	
Dec. 24th 1915 Do.	Short Route marches by Companies, with frequent halts to explain small tactical situations were carried out. Nothing further to record.	
Dec. 25th 1915 Do.	CHRISTMAS DAY — no parades. Nothing to record.	
Dec. 26th 1915 Do.	Short Route marches by Coys. A Court of Enquiry was held to enquire into the cause of wounds sustained by No. 8267 Pte: METCALFE D. on 11th inst. President: CAPT. W. HOLLAND. Members: 2/LT. W.B. VICKERS, 2/LT. L.S. DAVIS.	

WAR DIARY or INTELLIGENCE SUMMARY

Army Form C. 2118.

Hour, Date, Place	Summary of Events and Information	Remarks and references to Appendices
Dec: 27th 1915. L'ECLÈME. LE PREOL.	The Battn moved from REST BILLETS to LE PREOL, leaving L'ECLÈME at 8.50 a.m., & all ranks being billeted at LE PREOL before the midday meal. Weather – showery, mild. Nothing unusual to record. C.O. & O.C. Coys & M.G. Officer went to B1 Subsectn to reconnoitre.	
Dec: 28th 1915 LE PREOL. B1. SUBSECTn TRENCHES	The Battn moved up to the Trenches in B1 SUBSECTION, where we relieved the 17th R.F. guides from the latter regt. being at PONT FIXE at 11.50 a.m. Relief was reported complete by 1.30 p.m. The disposition of the battn: was as follows:–	See TRENCH MAP. 36 C N.W.1. 1/10.000.
	No 1 Coy. Right front Coy: 1 Platoon in RIGHT of FRONT LINE.	
	½ " " ARTILLERY ROW.	
	1 " " BAYSWATER	
	1½ " " SPOILBANK.	
	No 3 Coy. Left front Coy: 2 " " LEFT of FRONT LINE	
	2 " " ORCHARD REDOUBT	
	No 4 Coy. Support Coy. ½ " " SIDBURY HILL.	
	3½ " " PONT FIXE N.	
	No 2 Coy. Reserve Coy. remains in billets at LE PREOL, with Depot, Transport being at BEUVRY, for lack of horse standings at LE PREOL.	
	The right Coy is reached by means of CHEYNE WALK, & the left by ORCHARD ST. and BAKER ST. There is no communication between right & left Coys by day, except by going via PONT FIXE, as part of the front line is untenable, & STRATHCONA WALK & part of BAYSWATER are also impassable. Situation normal – nothing to record.	

WAR DIARY or INTELLIGENCE SUMMARY

Army Form C. 2118.

(Erase heading not required.)

Hour, Date, Place	Summary of Events and Information	Remarks and references to Appendices
Dec: 29th 1915. B1. SUBSECTION.	Weather fine – enemy quiet. Nothing of consequence to record. There is a well known enemy sniper behind a white cross on the far ~~side of the~~ canal bank on our right front. Much drainage work is necessary in the whole of the subsection, & it appears that this work must be started from the canal. Draining parties will therefore be put to work on clearing & deepening the various cuts from the CHEYNE WALK down to the Canal, & a party on the WILLOW RD. Drain, which is the main drain for the left section of the SUBSECTION. Telephonic communication is good all round. There is 1 phone in the Right front line, one in Left front line, one in Spoil Bank, or rather in CHEYNE WALK, just beyond SPOILBANK, & one in PONT FIXE N. We are also in communication with Reserve Coy via Brigade: also with Bns: on our right & left, & with 71st BTY. R.F.A., & 56th BTY. (HOWITZER).	
Dec: 30th 1915. B1 SUBSECTION.	Enemy continues quiet. Drainage work commenced last night has made an appreciable difference to CHEYNE WALK, & WILLOW RD drain is running well. Rations are brought by 1st line transport direct to PONT FIXE, & parties sent down from trenches for them. Rations arrive at PONT FIXE at 4.30 p.m.	

WAR DIARY
or
~~INTELLIGENCE SUMMARY~~.
(Erase heading not required.)

Army Form C. 2118.

Instructions regarding War Diaries and Intelligence Summaries are contained in F. S. Regs., Part II. and the Staff Manual respectively. Title pages will be prepared in manuscript.

Hour, Date, Place	Summary of Events and Information	Remarks and references to Appendices
Dec: 31st 1915 B1 SUBSECTION.	By order of G.O.C. our reserve Coy. has today moved up from billets at LE PREVOL to PONT FIXE, as the former place is considered too far away. It has been decided to carry on the drainage work by day, instead of by night, as this can now all be done under cover. For this reason only a small party was called up from No 2 Coy last night, & a party of about 100 has been at work today, along CHEYNE WALK and in BAYSWATER and SPOIL BANK, & about 20 men in ORCHARD REDOUBT. Enemy dropped a few small shells in PONT FIXE and along CHEYNE WALK, & also about OXFORD TERRACE, doing no damage. Situation remains normal.	

21st BATTALION

ROYAL FUSILIERS

JANUARY 1916

98th Brigade.
33rd Division.

WAR DIARY
or
INTELLIGENCE SUMMARY.
(Erase heading not required.)

Army Form C. 2118.

Hour, Date, Place	Summary of Events and Information	Remarks and references to Appendices
January 1st 1916. B1 SUBSECTION. & ANNEZIN.	The following casualties are reported as having occurred on Dec: 30th 1915 : 1 man killed, 4 wounded in action, and on Dec 31st, yesterday, 1 man wounded. The enemy celebrated the New Year by heavy shelling & rifle and machine gun fire.✕ Our own subsection did not receive much attention, but some damage was done in CHEYNE WALK, which was blocked in two or three places. We were able, however, to clear it in time for relief by 2nd Worcester Regt:, which commenced at 10.30 a.m., & was complete by 12.40 p.m. The Battn: then moving into billets at ANNEZIN, marching by way of southern canal bank - LE PREOL - BETHUNE. No casualties occurred. The two Coys from the firing line halted at LE PREOL for midday meals and baths, & the last of them was in billets at ANNEZIN by 6 p.m.	ANNEXE IV Ref BETHUNE Combined sheet E.9. ✕ between 11.30 p - 12.30 am night 31st/1st
Jan: 2nd 1916. ANNEZIN.	Nothing eventful has occurred today. The day has been spent in cleaning up equipment, clothing, etc. The M.G. Section, which was relieved today by guns of the 18th Mx: Regt: reported here at 7 p.m. O.C. this section, Lt. J.C. Jervis reported heavy shelling of B1 SUBSECTION during the day; the front line about the top of CHEYNE WALK appears to have suffered considerably, and also the latter trench itself. The Coy: of 2nd Worcesters in that part of the front line were forced to move over to their left, into that part part of the front line noted on	

# WAR DIARY or INTELLIGENCE SUMMARY.

Army Form C. 2118.

Instructions regarding War Diaries and Intelligence Summaries are contained in F.S. Regs., Part II. and the Staff Manual respectively. Title pages will be prepared in manuscript.

(Erase heading not required.)

Hour, Date, Place	Summary of Events and Information	Remarks and references to Appendices
Jan: 2nd 1916. ANNEZIN.	December 28th as untenable – the right of the line being held by our M.G. Section alone for some considerable time. The section suffered no casualties, & arrived here with all their guns complete. Lt. JERVIS brought news of heavy enemy shelling on FORT FIXE, HARLEY ST, and the CAMBRIN ROAD in which Lt: WOOD and several of our sister Battn, 19th R.F. appear to have been killed. Lt. WOOD is the first of the Officers of the two remaining PUBLIC SCHOOLS Battns: in the 98th Bde: to be killed.	
Jan: 3rd 1916 DITTO.	The Brigadier called at Battn: Hqrs: this afternoon and spoke to Major FENN. Nos 2 & 4 Coys: were inspected by Major FENN on parade and found clean and tidy. The C.O. inspected the billets of the Battn: in the forenoon. The A.D.M.S. 33rd Divn (Col: DALY) also inspected some of the billets, which are on the whole good. Latrines are excellent.	
Jan: 4th 1916 DITTO.	The C.O. inspected No 3 Coy on parade at 11.0 a.m. Major FENN inspected No 1 Coy and the M.G. Section on parade at 2.30 p.m. The A.D.V.S. 33rd Divn: (Major PLUNKETT) inspected the animals of 1st Line Transport during the afternoon. Nothing of note to record. Gas helmet practice was carried out.	
Jan: 5th 1916 DITTO.	Baths in ECOLE DE JEUNES FILLES, BETHUNE, & changes of under-clothing were at Battn's disposal today: all men had a bath and change. Orders were received to vacate ANNEZIN by 10 a.m. tomorrow, & all arrangements made – but these orders were cancelled, so we remain here until 7th inst.	

WAR DIARY or INTELLIGENCE SUMMARY

Army Form C. 2118.

(Erase heading not required.)

Hour, Date, Place	Summary of Events and Information	Remarks and references to Appendices
January 6th 1916. Ditto	Nothing to record. Arm drill & gas-helmet practice were carried out	
Jan: 7th 1916 BETHUNE	The Battn. marched from ANNEZIN to RUE D'AIRE, BETHUNE at 9.30 a.m. The C.O. & No. C. Companies went up to the Z Section of trenches to reconnoitre. The FIRST DRAFT to the Battn. of 23 NCOs & men arrived at 2.30 p.m., & was immediately told off to Nos 1 & 3 Companies, and fitted out ready to proceed to the trenches. Nothing unusual has occurred.	
Jan: 8th 1916 ANNEQUIN SOUTH.	The Battn. marched at 8.30 a.m. from BETHUNE to ANNEQUIN SOUTH, relieving 18th R.F. at the latter place. Nothing to record.	
Jan: 9th 1916. Ditto. Z¹ & Z² SUBSECTIONS TRENCHES	Orders were received to relieve 20th R.F. & one Coy. of R.W.F. in Z section of trenches at 8.30 a.m. tomorrow 10th. These orders were cancelled, & the relief ordered to take place commencing at 2 a.m. The relief was finally complete at 7 a.m. Delay was caused by guides from 20th R.F. for No 2 Company not turning up. This Coy. therefore had to make its own way to the front line without guides. The relief was otherwise carried out in good order, & without casualties.	

WAR DIARY or INTELLIGENCE SUMMARY

Army Form C. 2118.

Hour, Date, Place	Summary of Events and Information	Remarks and references to Appendices
January 10th 1916 Z SECTION TRENCHES.	Disposition of Battn in Trenches is as under:— No 3 Coy on RIGHT. (LEFT of Z² Subsection) No 2 " " R. CENTRE (R. of Z¹ ") No 4 " " L. " (CENTRE " ") No 1 " " LEFT (L. of " ") No. 1 Coy. of 19th (S) Battn Royal Fusiliers was left in reserve in WIMPOLE STREET. <u>Condition of the Trenches</u> — On the whole very good — communication trenches being entirely free from water. Some work, however, was found necessary in part of the Front Line between Boyau 14 and 17. A feature of these sections is the series of craters on the left which practically join up our lines with those of the Germans. There are 12 guns (6 Lewis 6 Machines) in this section of the line. Situation normal, nothing to record and no casualties — Weather fine.	?
January 10th 1916 Z(1) (Left Coy) } sub-section Z(2) } of trenches	Weather fine and mild — enemy quiet except for a little shelling of front and reserve lines, particularly the O P's, and MAISON ROUGE, near Battalion H Q's. It was found that the wire entanglements was very thin in places and much work will have to be done, especially by the Right Coy. Much wire was taken up to the	

WAR DIARY
or
INTELLIGENCE SUMMARY.
(Erase heading not required.)

Army Form C. 2118.

Instructions regarding War Diaries and Intelligence Summaries are contained in F.S. Regs., Part II. and the Staff Manual respectively. Title pages will be prepared in manuscript.

Hour, Date, Place	Summary of Events and Information	Remarks and references to Appendices
JANUARY 10th 1916 (Cont'd)	Front line to be made into "Footballs" and put out at night. Telephonic communication is also indifferent, the last battalion stationed here having apparently neglected the wire. There is no direct communication with right companies, but this is being put in hand. Much work was also done in cleaning out disused trenches and improving existing ones. The Left Coys. are in direct communication with 9th Batty R.F.A. the Left and Right Centre Coys. with 17th Batty R.F.A., but the Right Coy can only communicate with the 48th Batty. through the R.F.A. exchange. Casualties. One man wounded. Nothing to record.	
January 11th 1916.	Weather continuing fine and enemy quiet. Desultory shelling on both sides. No damage done to our trenches. Much work being done by wiring parties at night - improving parapets and fire steps by day - also opening up disused trenches. Casualties. One man killed, one wounded	
January 12th 1916	Still fine. Slight enemy artillery activity. Enemy rifle grenades and trench mortars in action on our Right Coys firing line. No casualties - Work continued as before. A Hun snipers post was destroyed by our artillery fire at A.21.b.6.0. A report was sent down from No. 4 Coy. at 2-0 a.m to the effect that 3 lights were seen by sentries in RUSSELL'S KEEP which appeared to be morse signals - position very difficult to locate owing to slight fog - direction	

WAR DIARY or **INTELLIGENCE SUMMARY.**

(Erase heading not required.)

Army Form C. 2118.

Hour, Date, Place	Summary of Events and Information	Remarks and references to Appendices
January 12th 1916 (Contd)	apparently S of CAMBRIN towards ANNEQUIN FOSSE. <u>Casualties</u> three men wounded	
January 13th 1916	Rather cooler, with some rain in afternoon. Enemy quiet except for a little French Mortar activity on left front. Work continued as before. Patrols out at night to make thorough inspection of enemy's wire. Officers patrol inspected half way round each side of GIBSON'S CRATER, finding no sign of enemy. Lights seen again in direction of ANNEQUIN FOSSE and reported on. <u>Casualties</u> NIL	
January 14th 1916	Weather cold and dull. Enemy artillery fairly active shelling front line and CAMBRIN. Our artillery put about 15 shells into a German working party on our left front with satisfactory results. Work continued as before. No lights reported previous night. <u>Casualties</u> NIL.	
January 15th 1916	Weather as before. Enemy quiet. About 1 p.m. MAISON ROUGE was shelled for about 15 minutes with 5.9 most of them exploding just over reserve trench by Battn HQs and 3 direct hits on MAISON ROUGE itself. ARTHUR'S KEEP also received attention from the enemy. Very bright moonlight night - patrols could not go out until 2.0 a.m. Enemy quiet. <u>Casualties</u> - 4 men wounded.	

WAR DIARY or INTELLIGENCE SUMMARY.

(Erase heading not required.)

Army Form C. 2118.

Hour, Date, Place	Summary of Events and Information	Remarks and references to Appendices
January 16th 1916. Z(1) Left } subsection of Z(2) } trenches	Weather dull and mild after very clear moonlight night patrols could not go out till 2 a.m. Enemy quiet both night & morning. Orders for relief of battalion as follows:- 2nd Argyll & Sutherland Highlanders to relieve 21st Royal Fusiliers less 1 Coy (No. 4 Coy) and 1 platoon (No. 5 platoon) - relief to commence at 4.30 - relieved parties to proceed via BURBURE ALLEY and CAMBRIN to old billets in ANNEQUIN SOUTH - parading by sections at 100 yards interval. No. 4 Coy under Capt J.V. Betts will be relieved at 2 p.m. and proceed to reserve line in WIMPOLE STREET taking over also LEWIS KEEP. No. 5 platoon under Lieut E. Thornton will relieve No. 12 platoon at 2 p.m. and form the garrison of ARTHURS KEEP, as the 2nd A & S. H. are not strong enough to take this over. All reliefs completed and battalion billeted at ANNEQUIN SOUTH by <u>Casualties</u> - One man killed.	
January 17th 1916 ANNEQUIN SOUTH.	Nothing of importance to report to-day - The day was spent in cleaning up clothing and equipment &c.	
January 18th 1916 ANNEQUIN SOUTH.	Nothing particular to record - Certain fatigue duties were carried out for R.E. The remainder of the battalion were engaged on improving dug-outs &c. The last draft of 30 N.C.O's & men were inspected by the G.O.C. <u>Casualties</u> - 1 man wounded	

WAR DIARY or **INTELLIGENCE SUMMARY**.
(Erase heading not required.)

Army Form C. 2118.

Hour, Date, Place	Summary of Events and Information	Remarks and references to Appendices
January 19th 1916 ANNEQUIN SOUTH	Nothing of importance to report. Battn engaged as on the 18th inst. Weather fine & mild.	
January 20th 1916 ANNEQUIN SOUTH	Nothing of importance to report. Battn engaged on fatigue work & repairing dug-outs & shelters &c. Baths for the ½ battalion were provided at ANNEQUIN FOSSE	
January 21st 1916 ANNEQUIN SOUTH	A draft of 30 N.C.O.'s and men reported about 10-30. This draft was inspected by Major Fenn & they were posted to Coys. Battalion engaged as on 20th inst.	
January 22nd 1916 ANNEQUIN SOUTH	Nothing of importance to record. Battn engaged on fatigue work & improving dug-outs & shelters. Weather fine.	
January 23rd 1916 BETHUNE	Weather very fine and clear. Enemy air-craft fairly active, 2 incendiary bombs dropped in billeting area (no damage). Battalion (less No. 4 Coy and No. 5 platoon) removed to reserve billets in RUE D'AIRE BETHUNE. Relief was ordered to commence at 3.0 p.m but was suspended for about an hour in consequence of the enemy shelling the LA BASSEE - BETHUNE Rd. - Battalion less No. 4 Coy and No. 5 platoon were all billeted in BETHUNE, the last party arriving about 8 p.m. Casualties 2/Lieut K.C. Horton was slightly wounded during progress of move. One man killed.	
January 24th 1916 BETHUNE.	No.4 Coy and No.5 platoon were relieved by 1 Coy Worcesters and 1 platoon 1st Queens respectively and proceeded to	

WAR DIARY or INTELLIGENCE SUMMARY.

(Erase heading not required.)

Army Form C. 2118.

Hour, Date, Place	Summary of Events and Information	Remarks and references to Appendices
24th January 1916 (Cont'd).	reserve billets in BETHUNE. The Machine Gun Section was also relieved. Secret instructions from 98th Bgde received as to steps to be taken in the event of the town being shelled.	
25th January 1916 BETHUNE	Weather fair & mild. Battalion engaged on fatigues, cleaning up clothing equipment &c. No 4 Coy and No. 5 platoon had baths at ECOLE DE JEUNES FILLES.	
26th January 1916 BETHUNE 3.30 pm Later.	Secret instructions as to Reserve Brigade Scheme received from 98th Bgde. (BM0 415 of 25-1-16) Wire received that the Brigade was under orders to move at one hour's notice until further orders. Orders issued making preparation for such move. Wire received to be prepared to move at short notice. Machine Gun section (two guns and crews) ordered to report at Bgde HQ's, which was done.	
27th January 1916 BETHUNE 11.35 am	Wire received that the Bgde was then at one hour's notice to move. Draft of 30 NCO's and men which joined on 21st inst. inspected by G.O.C. Weather - Dull and mild.	
28th January 1916 BETHUNE	CO and Company Commanders & MG Officer proceeded to B1 subsection trenches to reconnoitre in preparation for taking over that section of the line.	

WAR DIARY or ~~INTELLIGENCE SUMMARY.~~

(Erase heading not required.)

Army Form C. 2118.

Hour, Date, Place	Summary of Events and Information	Remarks and references to Appendices
Jan: 29th 1916. ff.	Still under orders to move at one hour's notice: wire received to "resume normal conditions" at about 2.30 p.m. Nothing of moment to report.	
Jan: 30th 1916. ff.	The Battn, under command of Major H. F. FENN relieved the 18th R.F. (Col: Lord Henry Scott) at 4.30 p.m. in B.1. Subsection. Relief reported complete, with exception of Machine Guns at 6.30 p.m. No casualties: nothing unusual to record. Lt. Col: J. Stuart-Wortley proceeded to England on 10 days leave of absence.	
Jan: 31st 1916. ff.	Nothing of moment. The Germans have planted a flag of the German colours about half-way across the no-man's-land in front of our RIGHT Company (No.1.) Weather fine & mild.	

98th Brigade.
33rd Division.

BATTALION went to G.H.Q. 29.2.16.

21st BATTALION

ROYAL FUSILIERS

FEBRUARY 1916

Hour, Date, Place	Summary of Events and Information	Remarks and references to Appendices
February 1st 1916. B1. Subsection Trenches.	The trenches in B1 Subsection are considerably drier than the last time we were in the same section, probably owing largely to the fact that level of comm has been considerably lowered, but also to improvement in the drainage system. The left of the line is not so much improved as the right – & indeed is in some respects not so good as before. BAKER ST, which was the principal communication trench at the beginning of last month, is now entirely disused, and FINCHLEY RD, which we did not then use, is now the only passable one: this is in parts very deep in mud & water – but it is hoped in a few days to make it dry. Work is required on gap in front line, on drainage generally, in BAYSWATER, OXFORD TERRACE, and on GUNNER TRENCH, where firesteps are to be built. 2 Patrols went out – one to capture flag mentioned above, (1 Sergt & 1 man), & an Officer's patrol of 2 n.c.o's & men under Capt. Whittington, R.H. The first patrol were captured by the enemy after taking down the flag. The second patrol, examining enemy wire, were surprised after mistaking their way, actually in the enemy wire. Capt Whittington & two men were apparently captured: Sergt L.N. JONES brought in the remaining 6 men safe, under M.G. & rifle fire from enemy. Two further patrols examining wire, report enemy wire very strong.	

WAR DIARY
or
INTELLIGENCE SUMMARY.

(Erase heading not required.)

Army Form C. 2118.

Instructions regarding War Diaries and Intelligence Summaries are contained in F.S. Regs., Part II. and the Staff Manual respectively. Title pages will be prepared in manuscript.

Hour, Date, Place	Summary of Events and Information	Remarks and references to Appendices
Feb: 2nd. 1916. B1. SUBSECTION TRENCHES.	Nothing of moment occurred during the day. Work in trenches being carried on satisfactorily. No patrols were sent out, as a British Searchlight was playing on the "No man's land".	
Feb: 3rd. 1916 Ditto.	Nothing of moment: weather colder with some rain. Patrols did not come in contact with enemy.	
Feb: 4th 1916.	All quiet. An Officers' patrol under 2/Lt. L.S. DAVIS went out on RIGHT of line, and encountered 3 GERMANS, who unfortunately escaped: they were pursued and 2/Lt. DAVIS was wounded. The patrol were forced by fire to give up pursuit, within a few yards of ENEMY WIRE, and returned without any further casualty.	
Feb: 5th 1916.	The parapet, at the junction of DEATH-OR-GLORY SAP with the FRONT LINE was blown in by enemy shell fire today. The machine Gunners in the SAP suffered 2 casualties, one killed and one wounded. An act of considerable merit in connection with this incident, was performed by No. 3259 Pte. SMITH C.H., a stretcher-bearer, who, learning that Corpl. NELSON was in the SAP severely wounded, cut his way through the debris of the entrance to the SAP, dressed	

WAR DIARY or ~~INTELLIGENCE SUMMARY~~.

Army Form C. 2118.

(Erase heading not required.)

Hour, Date, Place	Summary of Events and Information	Remarks and references to Appendices
Feb: 5th ctd.	the Corpl's wounds, and carried him back to safety - being exposed to considerable fire all the time. Pte SMITH was not wounded, but the Corpl: died an hour or so afterwards. Work on repairing the entrance to the Sap was begun after nightfall.	
Feb: 6th 1916. DITTO	Nothing unusual to report. Work on improvement to trenches & upkeep of same - also wiring being carried out as usual.	
Feb: 7th 1916. DITTO	Our artillery cut ENEMY WIRE in three places opposite our front, according to a preconceived plan, the ultimate object of which is a small raid on the ENEMY front line trenches by the TORTOISE which is to take place on the night of 8/9th, being carried out by BOMBERS and BAYONET-MEN. In the evening Lt. Col. E.B. DENISON, 1st K.R.R. arrived to take over command of this BATTALION, vice Lt. Col. J. STUART-WORTLEY.	
Feb: 8th 1916. DITTO	Nothing unusual to report. Observation of yesterdays cutting of wire by artillery fails to show any very considerable damage to enemy wire - our M.G's fired at intervals on the places where gaps or damage had been made by guns, to keep ENEMY WORKING parties away.	

WAR DIARY or ~~INTELLIGENCE SUMMARY~~.

(Erase heading not required.)

Army Form C. 2118.

Instructions regarding War Diaries and Intelligence Summaries are contained in F.S. Regs., Part II. and the Staff Manual respectively. Title pages will be prepared in manuscript.

Hour, Date, Place	Summary of Events and Information	Remarks and references to Appendices
Feb. 9th 1916. DITTO.	RAIDING PARTY which went out last night at 11.30 p.m. from DEATH or GLORY SAP, returned at 3.20 a.m. this morning: no casualties. Their scouts reported that the wire was not very badly damaged by our artillery, but that an enemy working party was engaged upon it: sentries were posted on enemy parapet, & were also patrolling behind their wire — so that entrance to the trenches was impossible. The party waited for some time & then Sergt. HASSELL, who was in command sent most of them back, while he and four others went forward, & dispersed the working party with bombs.	
Feb. 10th 1916 DITTO.	Nothing unusual to report. A company of the 7th LEINSTER REGT. came to the Battn: for "Company training", & relieved No. 2 Coy in the LEFT FRONT LINE. 2/Lt. J.C. CORNFORTH and 4 sergts from No. 3 Coy are attached to them to assist in instruction.	
Feb. 11th 1916	A Zeppelin was reported to have appeared at a considerable height over our lines steering WEST, at about 2.20 a.m. this morning. Zeppelins (probably 3) were also reported in neighbourhood of LOOS at 12.20 a.m.	

WAR DIARY or INTELLIGENCE SUMMARY.

(Erase heading not required.)

Army Form C. 2118.

Hour, Date, Place	Summary of Events and Information	Remarks and references to Appendices
Feb. 12th 1916. Ditto.	The Coy: of 7th Leicesters attached for training was relieved at 5.30pm this evening, by No 2 Coy from LE PREOL. No 4 Coy. in RIGHT front were relieved by No 1 Coy. from POINT FIXE at 6 p.m. Nothing unusual occurred.	
Feb: 13th 1916. Ditto.	The C.O. & Company Commanders of 16th K.R.R. who are to relieve us tomorrow came up to reconnoitre the line. Nothing to record.	
Feb: 14th 1916 Ditto & RUE D'AIRE BETHUNE.	The Battn was relieved by 16th K.R.R. during the evening, & marched to Billets in Rue d'Aire BETHUNE. Nothing unusual occurred.	
Feb: 15th 1916 RUE D'AIRE BETHUNE.	All ranks are employed in cleaning up. Nothing to record.	
Feb: 16th 1916 Ditto.	A farewell message was received last night from Lt. Col. T. STUART-WORTLEY, lately in command of the Battalion. By order of the present	

WAR DIARY or INTELLIGENCE SUMMARY.

Army Form C. 2118.

Instructions regarding War Diaries and Intelligence Summaries are contained in F.S. Regs., Part II. and the Staff Manual respectively. Title pages will be prepared in manuscript.

(Erase heading not required.)

Hour, Date, Place	Summary of Events and Information	Remarks and references to Appendices
Feb 16th 1916 (Ctd.)	Commanding Officer this was published as a Special Order. The C.O. inspected the last Draft, which arrived on the 14th inst. The C.O. also inspected the men's Billets, finding them clean & tidy.	
Feb 17th 1916 Ditto.	The Battn had the use of the Baths at Essars les Tourez Mines today; all were bathed and received clean clothes.	
Feb 18th 1916. Ditto.	Nothing to record; over 300 men employed on R.E. fatigues.	
Feb 19th 1916 Ditto.	The C.O. inspected each company on parade today for the first time since taking over command of the Battalion. Weather very cold with some rain.	
Feb 20th 1916 Ditto.	German Aeroplanes dropped several Bombs on BETHUNE about 11 - midnight last night. Only material damage appears to have been done & that very slight. Day spent mainly on R.E. Fatigues - over 300 men being employed on this work.	

WAR DIARY
or
INTELLIGENCE SUMMARY.
(Erase heading not required.)

Army Form C. 2118.

Instructions regarding War Diaries and Intelligence Summaries are contained in F.S. Regs., Part II. and the Staff Manual respectively. Title pages will be prepared in manuscript.

Hour, Date, Place	Summary of Events and Information	Remarks and references to Appendices
February 21st 1916. DITTO.	The Draft of NCOs & men which joined the Bn on the 16th inst. was inspected today by the acting Brigadier 98th Bde (Col. Rowley, 1st M'x) R.E. Fatigues again employed over 100 men.	
Feb. 22nd 1916 DITTO, and ANNEQUIN SOUTH.	The Battalion moved from BETHUNE to ANNEQUIN SOUTH, relieving the 1st Bn. Middlesex Regt. at 5 p.m. Nothing unusual to record.	
Feb 23rd 1916 DITTO and Z.2 SUBSECT. TRENCHES.	The Bn. relieved the 2nd A. & S. Highlanders in Z.2. Subsection Trenches this evening. Relief carried out without casualty.	
Feb 24th 1916 Z.2. SUBSECTION TRENCHES.	Nothing of moment to record. One man of No 2 Company, killed.	
Feb 25th DITTO.	One man of No 2 wounded. Nothing to record.	
Feb 26th DITTO	Weather intensely cold — with snow showers. One man killed and two wounded: all of No 3 Company. Lt. Col. E.B. Denison proceeded on leave at midnight.	

WAR DIARY
or
INTELLIGENCE SUMMARY.
(Erase heading not required.)

Army Form C. 2118.

Instructions regarding War Diaries and Intelligence Summaries are contained in F.S. Regs., Part II. and the Staff Manual respectively. Title pages will be prepared in manuscript.

Hour, Date, Place	Summary of Events and Information	Remarks and references to Appendices
February 26th 1916. DITTO.	for 10 days; Major H.F. FENN returned from leave, and took over temporary command of the Battalion.	
Feb. 27th 1916. DITTO.	Nothing to record. The C.O. & Co. Companies of the 4th KINGS (L'pool) Regt. who are relieving us tomorrow came up to reconnoitre the line.	
Feb. 28th 1916 DITTO and RUE D'AIRE BETHUNE.	The Battn. was relieved by the 4th KINGS, relief being reported complete by 8 p.m. The Battn. marched to billets in BETHUNE — a somewhat arduous march after the bitter weather we have experienced during the last six days in the trenches. — As the Battalion leaves the brigade, & moves out of the fighting line tomorrow, in order to supply some 400 men required for promotion to commissioned rank, the following farewell message received from the Brigadier General commanding 9th Brigade is of considerable interest:—	

WAR DIARY
~~INTELLIGENCE SUMMARY.~~
(Erase heading not required.)

Army Form C. 2118.

Hour, Date, Place	Summary of Events and Information	Remarks and references to Appendices
Feb. 29th 1916. C/o BETHUNE (from Z.2. Subsec^{tn})	"It is with regret that I am losing your services "from the Brigade, but in the interest of the Army "generally it is necessary that you should be "withdrawn for a time, to enable the large "number of men who are recommended for "Commissions to be dealt with. "Since you have been in France you have "experienced very considerable hardships in "the trenches, and have been under heavy "fire. The former you have borne cheerfully "and under the latter you have acquitted "yourselves with credit. The conduct of the "Battalion has been excellent, as was to have "been expected of you. The experience thus "gained will, I hope, prove of great value "to all ranks especially those who may "be raised to commissioned rank. "Should you not return to this Brigade, you "take with you my very best wishes for your "future." Signed E.P. Strickland Brigadier-Genl. Com^{dg} 98th Inf. Bde.	

WAR DIARY or INTELLIGENCE SUMMARY.

(Erase heading not required.)

Army Form C. 2118.

Hour, Date, Place	Summary of Events and Information	Remarks and references to Appendices
February 29th 1916 BETHUNE & WARDRECQUES (G.H.Q)	The Battn. left BETHUNE by train for WARDRECQUES in the G.H.Q. area at 1.19 p.m., arriving at ST. OMER Station between 4 & 5 p.m. Motor Omnibuses to convey the men to WARDRECQUES eventually arrived at 6 p.m. & the men were billeted by 9.0 p.m.